Counting the Poor in India

C. Rangarajan is a leading economist of India who has played a key role both as an academic and a policy maker. He has held several important positions which include Governor of Reserve Bank of India; Chairman, Economic Advisory Council to the Prime Minister; Governor of the state of Andhra Pradesh; and Chairman, Twelfth Finance Commission. Dr Rangarajan was Governor of the Reserve Bank of India during 1992-1997 when India embarked on wide-ranging economic reforms. He was President of the Indian Economic Association in 1988 and President of the Indian Econometric Society in 1994. He was awarded Padma Vibhusan in 2002. He is currently Chairman, Madras School of Economics and Chancellor of the University of Hyderabad.

S. Mahendra Dev has been the Director and Vice Chancellor, Indira Gandhi Institute of Development Research (IGIDR) in Mumbai, since 2010. Prior to this position, he was Chairman of the Commission for Agricultural Costs and Prices, Ministry of Agriculture from 2008 to 2010. He was Director, Centre for Economic and Social Studies, Hyderabad, for 9 years from 1999 to 2008. He is member of the Board of Trustees of International Food Policy Research Institute (IFPRI), Washington, D.C. He was Acting Chairman of the National Statistical Commission, Government of India. He received his PhD from the Delhi School of Economics and did his postdoctoral research at Yale University. His main areas of interest are: development economics, macro and agriculture policies, employment, poverty, inequality and, social sector. He received Malcolm Adisesaiah Award for outstanding work on development studies.

Counting the Poor in India

Where Do We Stand

INCLUDES:
REPORT OF THE EXPERT GROUP TO REVIEW
THE METHODOLOGY FOR MEASUREMENT OF POVERTY

C. RANGARAJAN
S. MAHENDRA DEV

ACADEMIC FOUNDATION
NEW DELHI

www.academicfoundation.org

First published in 2017
by

ACADEMIC FOUNDATION
4772-73 / 23 Bharat Ram Road, (23 Ansari Road),
Darya Ganj, New Delhi - 110 002 (India).
Phones : 23245001 / 02 / 03 / 04.
Fax : +91-11-23245005.
E-mail : books@academicfoundation.com
www.academicfoundation.org

Disclaimer:
The findings/views/opinions expressed in this book are solely those of the author and do not necessarily reflect the views of the publisher.

Cataloging in Publication Data--DK
Courtesy: D.K. Agencies (P) Ltd. <docinfo@dkagencies.com>

Rangarajan, C. (Chakravarthy), 1932- **author.**
Counting the poor in India : where do we stand / C. Rangarajan, S. Mahendra Dev.
pages cm
ISBN 9789332703834

1. Poverty--India--Measurement. 2. Poverty--Government policy--India. I. Mahendra Dev, S., author. II. Title.

HC440.P6R36 2017 DDC 339.460954 23

Typeset, printed and bound by The Book Mint, New Delhi.
www.thebookmint.in

CONTENTS

Acknowledgement

A major part of this book contains the Report of the Expert Group to Review the Methodology for Measurement of Poverty which was set up in 2012. Besides the authors, the other members of the Committee were Prof K. Sundaram, Shri Mahesh Vyas and Shri K.L. Datta. We gratefully acknowledge their contribution and in a sense this book is as much theirs as ours. We thank the Editors of *Economic and Political Weekly* and *Indian Express* for permitting us to include the articles published in their Journals. Finally, we thank Prof S. Chandrasekhar of IGIDR for providing some of the estimates from NSS data used in some sections of this book.

Introduction

To review and take a fresh look at the methodology for measurements of poverty, the Government of India appointed an Expert Group in June 2012.[1] Both the authors were associated with the Group. This book contains the Report of the Expert Group (which is not otherwise easily accessible) and four other articles which were written subsequently to explain some of the issues that were raised after the publication of the Report.

Measurement of Poverty

There is a considerable amount of debate on how to measure poverty. Among the many approaches for measuring poverty, prescribing a minimum level of income or consumption expenditure for defining poverty appears to be the most appropriate method. Any household failing to meet this level of consumption expenditure can be treated as a poor household. This minimum level of consumption expenditure can be derived, in turn, in terms of minimum expenditure on food and non-food items. The poverty ratio is measured from an exogenously determined poverty line quantified in terms of per capita consumption expenditure over a month and the class distribution of persons obtained from the large sample survey of consumer expenditure data of the National Sample Survey Office (NSSO).

What is the rationale for having poverty estimates based on consumption estimates? First, in the minds of most people, being rich or poor is associated with levels of income. The various non-income indicators of poverty are in fact reflections of inadequate

1. Expert Group to Review the Methodology for Measurement of Poverty. The report was released in June 2014.

income. Defining poverty in terms of income or in the absence of such data in terms of expenditure seems more appropriate, and it is this method that is followed in most countries.

Some analysts argue for multidimensional approach for measuring poverty. The search for non-income dimensions of poverty possibly stems from a view that, the 'capabilities', may not be tightly linked to the privately purchased consumption basket in terms of which the poverty lines are currently drawn. Therefore, poverty based on income or consumption is different from deprivations based on education or health. The multidimensional indicators/measures raise several issues regarding their measurability, aggregation across indicators and crucially, of data bases that provide the requisite information at reasonably short intervals. One is not against multidimensional poverty or deprivations. The progress of non-income indicators like education, health, situation, drinking water, child mortality etc. can be monitored over time along with income or consumption poverty. But, aggregating them into an index would have several problems as indicated above.

In using the level of private consumption expenditure as the criterion for measuring poverty, there are two aspects which need to be noted. The poverty ratio derived from such a method which is also called the HCR (head count ratio), does not give an idea of the depth of poverty. An analysis of the distribution of the people below poverty line is also needed. However, our own study in relation to India shows that bulk of the people counted as poor hover around the poverty line. Second, poverty line estimates using private consumption expenditures do not take into account the benefits accruing to various sections of society from public expenditures. Public expenditures on social sectors like health and education on per capita basis have been increasing in real terms. However, the distribution of public expenditures decile-wise is not available. Nevertheless, it is safe to assume that bulk of the benefits from public expenditures on basic needs like primary health and primary education accrue to lower deciles of population. Therefore, in revaluing the level of poverty overtime, we need to keep this consideration in mind.

Key Improvements

The methodology to measure poverty has been the subject matter of many committees appointed by the erstwhile Planning Commission. The original methodology evolved by Y.K. Alagh in 1979 has been modified by the Expert Group (Lakdawala) in 1993 and then by the Expert Group (Tendulkar) in 2009. The Tendulkar Committee recommendations evoked a raging debate. In this context to take another look at the methodology of measuring poverty, as mentioned earlier, a new expert group was appointed (C. Rangarajan as Chairman) in 2012, and the group submitted its report towards the end of June 2014. In substance, the Tendulkar Committee's poverty line and Rangarajan Committee's poverty line are of the same class. But, Rangarajan Committee has made the following improvements over Tendulkar committee's poverty line.

The Expert Group (Tendulkar) did not construct a new poverty basket. It adopted the officially measured urban poverty line of 2004-05 based on Expert Group (Lakdawala) methodology. This poverty line was used to derive the state level rural and urban poverty. The Committee provided no justification as to why the all India urban poverty line was correctly estimated. In addition, this was a departure from the earlier practice of using two separate poverty line baskets for rural and urban areas. The Expert Group (Rangarajan) reverts to the practice of having separate all-India rural and urban poverty basket lines and deriving state-level rural and urban estimates from these.

The Expert Group (Tendulkar) had decided not to anchor the poverty line to the then available official calorie norms used in all poverty estimations since 1979. However, on a review of subsequent research, the Expert Group (Rangarajan) took a considered view that deriving the food component of the poverty line basket by reference to the simultaneous satisfaction of all three nutrient-norms is appropriate. The Rangarajan Committee computed the average requirements of calories, proteins and fats based on Indian Council of Medical Research (ICMR) norms differentiated by age, gender and activity for all-India rural and urban regions to derive the minimum normative levels of nourishment. Accordingly, the energy requirement works out to 2,155 kcal per person per day in rural areas and 2,090 kcal per person per day in urban areas. The Rangarajan Committee views the calorie norm not as a single number but as an average in a band of +/-10 per cent of these values and with intakes even at the lower end still being adequate enough not to adversely affect health and work. The protein and fat requirements have been estimated on the same lines as for energy. A food basket that simultaneously meets all the normative requirements of the three nutrients defines the food component of the poverty line basket proposed by the Expert Group (Rangarajan). These nutrient norms are met for persons located in the sixth fractile (25-30%) in rural areas and for those in the fourth fractile (15-20%) in urban areas in 2011-12.

The median fractile (45-50%) values of clothing expenses, rent, conveyance and education expenses are treated as the normative requirements of the basic non-food expenses of clothing, housing, mobility and education of a poverty line basket. This works out to ₹141 per capita per month in rural areas and ₹407 in urban areas. The observed expenses of all other non-food expenses of the fractile classes that meet these requirements are considered as part of the poverty line basket. This works out to ₹277 per capita per month in rural areas and ₹344 in urban areas. The new poverty line thus works out to monthly per capita consumption expenditure of ₹972 in rural areas and ₹1,407 in urban areas in 2011-12. For a family of five, this translates into a monthly consumption expenditure of ₹4,860 in rural areas and ₹7,035 in urban areas.

One should choose that poverty line which reflects a carefully calculated minimum level of food and non food requirements. Rangarajan Committee computed a fresh basket in the light of the most recently available minimum requirements of food. It did not simply update an earlier basket using price indices. Also for the first time, minimum non-food requirements for certain categories were included in determining the basket.

Usefulness of Poverty Line

Another issue is the usefulness of the computed poverty ratios. The erstwhile Planning Commission had earlier decided to delink the consumption based poverty estimates for allocating resources to states. What is the purpose of NSS consumption-based estimates if they are not used for the allocation of funds and capping beneficiaries under government programmes? These poverty ratios are really to be used basically to assess the changes in poverty at national and state levels, or at the district level. This will be useful for creating appropriate policies. For example, one can examine changes in poverty in different phases of the post-reform period to understand what impact anti-poverty programmes, in conjunction with growth, have had on poverty. Poverty ratios are not used for identification of the individual poor, which is necessary to ensure that the benefits of programmes and schemes reach only the deserving and targeted group. The Expert Group (Rangarajan) deliberated on the issue of use of poverty ratio for determining the eligibility and entitlements for a wide range of poverty alleviation programmes and social welfare schemes implemented by various Ministries and Departments of the Government of India in association with the State governments. The Group recommended that the beneficiaries under target group oriented schemes of the Government may be selected from the deprivation-specific ranking of households. Such ranking of households could be generated for a large number of indicators representing deprivation and levels of living for which the information has been gathered at the household and individual level in the Socio-Economic Caste Census (SECC)-2011 and population census. The beneficiaries could be selected from this set of households until the resources earmarked for the programme/scheme permit.

Policy Implications

The mandate of the Group did not require it to suggest measures for reducing poverty. However, a quick survey of the poverty ratios over time indicates a two-fold approach to ameliorate poverty. First, growth is important. There are indications that poverty ratios come down faster during periods of higher growth. Growth can help to reduce poverty in two ways. As growth occurs, it does affect all sections of the society. As the saying goes arising tide lifts all boats. However the extent to which the bottom deciles of the population will benefit will depend upon how fast the growth is, and what the composition of that growth is. A strong growth also increases the resources available to the public authorities and this will enable them to increase the social sector expenditures. It is, however, obvious that the very fact that poverty ratio still hovers around 30 per cent means that growth by itself will not be adequate to reduce poverty. It is necessary to launch specific programmes which go to directly help poorer groups and vulnerable sections.

1

Counting the Poor

Measurement and Other Issues

Introduction

Growth is not the sole objective of economic policy. It is necessary to ensure that the benefits of growth accrue to all sections of the society. Eradication of poverty is thus an important objective. Human beings need a certain minimum consumption of food and non-food items to survive. However, the perception regarding what constitutes poverty varies over time and across countries. Nevertheless, there is need for a measure of poverty. Only then, it will be possible to evaluate how the economy is performing in terms of providing a certain minimum standard of living to all its citizens. Measurement of poverty has, therefore, important policy implications.

There are in fact many approaches for measuring poverty. Some analysts focus on deprivations of people in terms of health, education, sanitation or housing. There are, however, many problems associated with this approach including difficulties in aggregating deprivations on several scores derived from different sources. Perhaps the best approach is look at it in terms of certain minimum consumption expenditure per person or preferably per household. Any household failing to meet this level of consumption expenditure can be treated as a poor household. This minimum level of consumption expenditure can be derived, in turn, in terms of minimum expenditure on food and non-food items. The poverty ratio, which is the ratio of number of poor to the total population is expressed as percentage. It is also known as HCR (head-count ratio). The poverty ratio is measured from an exogenously determined poverty line quantified in terms of per capita consumption expenditure over a month and the class distribution of persons obtained from the large sample survey of consumer expenditure data of the National Sample Survey Office (NSSO).

In India, we have had a long history of studies on measurement of poverty.[1] The methodology for estimation of poverty used by the Planning Commission has been based on the recommendations made by Working Group/Task Force/Expert Groups consisting of eminent experts in the field. The Planning Commission has constituted these Groups from time to time to revisit the methodological issues related to the measurement of poverty so as to make the estimates more relevant to the contemporary economic situation. After the Working Group of the Planning Commission delineated the methodology of poverty estimation in 1962, it has been intensely debated by the academicians, experts, policy planners, etc., over the years. In response, the Planning Commission has constituted Task Force/ Expert Group from time to time to review the methodology. These include the Task Force under the chairmanship of Y.K. Alagh in 1977; the Expert Groups under the chairmanship of D.T. Lakdawala in 1989 and S.D. Tendulkar in 2005.

In June 2012, the Government of India (GoI) appointed an Expert Group (C. Rangarajan as Chairman) to take a fresh look at the methodology for the measurement of poverty. The Committee submitted its report towards the end of June 2014. The purpose of this article is to briefly explain the approach taken by this Expert Group (Rangarajan) and also to clarify some of the issues raised by few researchers and others on the report recently.

Approaches of the Earlier Committees

The Planning Commission is the nodal agency in the GoI for estimation of poverty and these estimates are based on the recommendations of the committees appointed by it. Before going to the Expert Group (Rangarajan), the approaches of earlier committees on estimation of poverty are described below.

1. Srinivasan (2007) reviews the evolution of poverty lines in India from a historical perspective and critically discusses some issues relating to official poverty lines. Srinivasan (2013), among other things, discusses about poverty lines in India in the recent past.

The Working Group 1962 recommended that the national minimum consumption expenditure for a household of five persons (four adult consumption units) should not be less than ₹100 per month or ₹20 per capita per month in terms of 1960-61 prices. For urban areas, this figure was ₹125 per month or ₹25 per capita per month to cover the higher prices there. The poverty line excluded expenditure on health and education, both of which, it was assumed, were to be provided by the State. The Working Group (1962) appeared to have taken into account the recommendation of balanced diet made by the Nutrition Advisory Group of the Indian Council of Medical Research (ICMR) in 1958. This poverty line was widely used in the 1960s and 1970s to estimate the poverty ratio at national and state level.

Task Force 1979 (Alagh) (GoI, 1979) estimated average calorie requirements and the poverty line corresponding to the calorie requirement. The estimated calorie norm was 2400 kcal per capita per day in rural areas and 2100 kcal per capita per day in urban areas. To work out the monetary equivalent of these norms, 28th Round (1973-74) NSS data relating to household consumption both in quantitative and value terms were used. Based on the observed consumer behaviour in 1973-74 it was estimated that, on an average, consumer expenditure (food and non-food) of ₹49.09 per capita per month was associated with a caloric intake of 2400 per capita per day in rural areas and ₹56.64 per capita per month with a calorie intake of 2100 per day in urban areas. The NSS distribution of private consumption was adjusted pro-rata to correspond to the consumption estimates of National Accounts Statistics (NAS) made by the Central Statistical Office (CSO). Using the poverty line and the adjusted distribution of persons by expenditure classes for the reference year the percentage of persons below the poverty line was estimated. The poverty line defined by the Task Force at 1973-74 prices was updated by the Planning Commission (to estimate poverty for a later year) using the implicit Central Statistical Office (CSO) private consumption expenditure deflator.

Planning Commission appointed Expert Group (Lakdawala) in 1989 which submitted its report in 1993 (GoI, 1993). The Expert

Group (Lakdawala) did not redefine the poverty line. It retained the one defined by the Task Force (Alagh) which was at national level in rural and urban areas. It disaggregated these national poverty lines into state-specific poverty lines in order to reflect the inter-state price differentials measured by Fisher's index. These state-specific poverty lines of base year (1973-74) were updated for subsequent years by using Consumer Price Index for Agricultural Labourers (CPIAL) for rural areas and Consumer Price Index for Industrial Workers (CPIIW) for urban areas. Two factors largely distinguish the Expert Group (Lakdawala) methodology of poverty estimation from those of the Task Force (Alagh). First, the Expert Group (Lakdawala) method uses state-specific poverty lines as against national poverty line for estimation of poverty in the state; it thereby captures the cost of living in the states more accurately (as compared to the Task Force method). Second, the Expert Group (Lakdawala) uses the state-wise consumption distribution of the NSS without any adjustment to the NAS consumption. This is a major departure from the Task Force method, which did this adjustment on a pro-rata basis.

The Expert Group under the chairmanship of Suresh D. Tendulkar was constituted by the Planning Commission in December 2005. This group submitted its report in November 2009 (GoI, 2009). The Expert Group (Tendulkar) did not construct a poverty line. It adopted the officially measured urban poverty line of 2004-05 based on Expert Group (Lakdawala) methodology and converted this poverty line (which is URP-consumption based) into MRP-consumption.[2] The Expert Group (Tendulkar) method of estimation of poverty is described in the following three steps:

Step 1: Convert the URP-consumption based urban poverty line into MRP-consumption based poverty line. Here, the MRP-consumption based urban poverty line is worked out as the level of per capita consumption expenditure in the MRP

2. URP-consumption=consumption data are collected from the households using 30 day recall period for all the items. MRP-consumption=consumption data for five non-food items viz., clothing, footwear, durable goods, education, and institutional medical expenses are collected using 365-day recall period and 30-day recall period for the remaining items.

consumption distribution that corresponds to the bottom 25.7 per cent of the population.

Step 2: State-specific urban poverty lines are derived from the (MRP-consumption based) national urban poverty line using urban state-relative-to-all-India Fisher indices.[3]

Step 3: The state-specific rural poverty lines are worked out from the state-specific urban poverty lines by applying within-state rural-relative-to-urban Fisher indices.[4]

Here, the state index numbers relative to the all-India numbers and the state-specific rural prices relative to the state-specific urban prices are computed from the implicit price indices derived from the quantity and value of different items of consumer expenditure gathered in the NSS consumption expenditure.

Urban poverty is same for both expert groups (Lakdawala and Tendulkar) at 25.7 per cent in 2004-05. However, the all-India rural poverty ratio at 41.8 per cent is one and a half times the estimate of Expert Group (Lakdawala) which was 28.3 per cent in the same year as Expert Group (Tendulkar) uses urban basket for rural areas.

Suggested Methodology by Expert Group (Rangarajan)

The high rate of increase in per capita income and consumption in the first decade of this century and the consequential changes in the structure of the economy as well as in people's perspectives on poverty was viewed as requiring a fresh look at the poverty line

---

3. This national level urban poverty line is disaggregated into state-specific poverty lines using "urban state-relative-to-all-India" price differentials. The prices differentials are constructed from a variety of price data most of which are implicit. For 15 commodity groups namely, cereals, pulses, milk, oil, egg-fish-meat, vegetables, fresh fruit, dry-fruit, sugar, salt-spices, other-food, intoxicants, fuel-light, clothing & bedding and footwear, the Fisher indices are computed using implicit prices obtained from the NSS consumer expenditure data of 61st Round (2004-05); for five item groups namely entertainment, personal care items, miscellaneous goods, miscellaneous services and durables, Labour Bureau price data underlying CPIAL and CPIIW is used. The pricing of educational services are constructed from the employment-unemployment survey of the NSS 61st Round (2004-05) and of health services are constructed from the health and morbidity survey of NSS 60th Round (January-June 2004).

4. The state-specific rural poverty lines (of 2004-05) are worked out by adjusting the state-specific urban poverty lines (of 2004-05) with the "within-state-rural-relative-to-urban"price differentials computed from the similar price statistics as in the case of disaggregating the national poverty line into state-specific poverty lines in urban areas.

and its composition. Along-side, significant changes have occurred in the composition of private consumption expenditure: a reduction in the share of food, of foodgrains within food and of cereals within foodgrains.

It is against this background that the Expert Group (Rangarajan) has to define its methodology for drawing up the poverty line and the measurement of poverty.[5] In the past, the Planning Commission had constituted Expert Groups after a gap of about 12 to 15 years. However, Expert Group (Rangarajan) has been constituted less than three years after the submission of its recommendations of Expert Group (Tendulkar) and only one and a half years after the acceptance of its recommendations by the Planning Commission. The apparent urgency with which the Expert Group (Rangarajan) has been formed reflects a need to examine the estimation of poverty in India keeping in mind the changed aspirations regarding the minimally acceptable standards of living in the country.

The first step in measurement of poverty involves determining the PLB (poverty line basket) of goods and services and the associated level of monthly per capita (total) private consumption expenditure as captured by the NSS Consumer Expenditure Surveys. The Expert Group opted for Modified Mixed Recall Period (MMRP) reference period while Expert Group (Tendulkar) considered Mixed Recall Period (MRP) reference period consumption expenditure for

5. The Expert Group (Rangarajan) has the following terms of reference:

(a) "To comprehensively review the existing methodology of estimation of poverty and examine whether the poverty line should be fixed solely in terms of a consumption basket or whether other criteria are also relevant, and if so, whether the two can be effectively combined to evolve a basis for estimation of poverty in rural and urban areas.

(b) "To examine the issue of divergence between consumption estimates based on the NSSO methodology and those emerging from the National Accounts aggregates; and to suggest a methodology for updating consumption poverty lines using the new consumer price indices launched by the CSO for rural and urban areas state-wise.

(c) "To review alternative methods of estimation of poverty which may be in use in other countries, including their procedural aspects; and indicate whether on this basis, a particular method can be evolved for empirical estimation of poverty in India, including procedures for updating it over time and across states.

(d) "To recommend how the estimates of poverty, as evolved above, should be linked to eligibility and entitlements for schemes and programmes under the Government of India".

estimation of poverty.[6] Experts of Rangarajan group are of the view that the mix of reference periods for different items underlying the MMRP-estimates may be expected to yield estimates that are closer to their true value. Further, in all future NSS Consumer Expenditure Surveys only the MMRP estimates will be available. It automatically implies that deriving poverty estimates using MMRP distribution is not possible for all years prior to 2009-10.

In defining the new consumption basket separating the poor from the rest, the Expert Group (Rangarajan) is of the considered view that it should contain a food component that addresses the capability to be adequately nourished as well as some normative level of consumption expenditure for essential non-food item groups (education, clothing, conveyance and house rent) besides a residual set of behaviourally determined non-food expenditure.

As a first step towards defining the food component of the poverty line basket, the Expert Group (Rangarajan) has recomputed the average requirements of calories, proteins and fats, per-capita per-day at the all-India level for 2011-12, separately for the rural and the urban populations. This is based on ICMR norms differentiated by age, gender and activity for all-India rural and urban regions to derive the normative levels of nourishment. Accordingly, the energy requirement works out to 2,155 kcal per person per day in rural areas and 2,090 kcal per person per day in urban areas. Based on some studies, it is, however, more appropriate to treat the normal calorie requirements to be within a range of +/- 10 per cent of these values and the lower level of such a range to be adequate enough to not adversely affect health.[7] The protein and fat requirements have been estimated on the same lines as for energy. These requirements are 48 gms and 28 gms per capita per day, respectively, in rural areas; and 50 gms and 26 gms per capita per day in urban areas.

---

6. In the MMRP, the consumer expenditure data is gathered from the households using the recall period of: (a) 365-days for clothing, footwear, education, institutional medical care, and durable goods, (b) 7-days for edible oil, egg, fish and meat, vegetables, fruits, spices, beverages, refreshments, processed food, *pan*, tobacco and intoxicants, and (c) 30-days for the remaining food items, fuel and light, miscellaneous goods and services including non-institutional medical, rents and taxes.

7. see Sukhatme (1981), Meenakshi and Viswanathan (2013).

A food basket that simultaneously meets all the norms for the three nutrients, with the calorie-norm being satisfied at least at the lower level of the range defines the food component of the poverty line basket proposed by the Expert Group (Rangarajan). The latest information on class distribution of nutrient-intake, based on estimates of food consumption on MMRP, is available for the year 2011-12 (NSS 68th Round). It is seen that the nutrient-intake norms, including the calorie–norms at the lower end of the range, are met for the persons located in the sixth fractile (25-30%) in rural areas and for those in the fourth fractile (15-20%) in urban areas. The average monthly per capita consumption expenditure on food in these fractile classes is ₹554 in rural areas and ₹656 in urban areas.

The non-food component of the PLB has both a normative component and, a component given by the observed consumption pattern of households in the fractile-group in which the food–component of the PLB is located. The normative component relates to the private consumption expenditure aimed at capabilities in respect of education, clothing, shelter (rent) and mobility (conveyance). Since it is difficult to set minimum norms for these essential non-food items, the Expert Group (Rangarajan) recommends that observed expenditures on these items by households located in the median fractile (45-50 percentile) be treated as the normative minimum private consumption expenditure on these items. For all other non-food goods and services, the observed expenditure of that fractile-class which meets the nutrient-norms (the 25th-30th percentile in rural India and the 15th-20th percentile in urban India) is taken to define the PLB in respect of these items.

The MPCE (monthly per capita consumption expenditure) which constitutes new poverty line basket, separately in rural and urban areas, is given in Table 1.1.

The MPCE of ₹972 (554+141+277) in rural areas and ₹1,407 (656+407+344) in urban areas constitute the new poverty lines at the all-India level as per the recommendation of the Expert Group (Rangarajan). They translate to a monthly per household expenditure of ₹4,860 in rural India and of ₹7,035 for urban India—assuming a family of 5-members in each case.

Table 1.1

Consumption Expenditure of PLB in Rural Areas and Urban Areas (2011-12)

(*MPCE in ₹*)

Items	*Rural*		*Urban*	
	Sixth Fractile (25-30%)	*Median Class (45-50%)*	*Fourth Fractile (15-20%)*	*Median Class (45-50%)*
Food	554	678	656	977
Four essential non-food items	102	141	181	407
Other non-food items	277	347	344	571
Total MPCE	933	1166	1181	1955
MPCE-Poverty Line	972		1407	

Source: Derived from NSS Consumer Expenditure Survey 2011-12, 68th Round.

Estimations of poverty line made for the Expert Group (Rangarajan) based on independent large survey of households by CMIE and using a different methodology wherein a household is considered poor if it is unable to save, yield results that are remarkably close to those derived using the NSSO data. This provides additional evidence to the poverty line derived by the Expert Group. However, the alternative approach can be established only when NSSO initiates surveys on income and expenditure as recommended by the Committee to Review the Methodology for the Estimation of Savings and Investment.

We can look at the proposed poverty line level in terms of PPP dollars per capita per day. As per the most recent (World Bank, 2014) PPP–values, the poverty line translates to $2.14 per capita per day for rural India, $3.10 per capita per day for urban India and $2.44 per capita per day for the country as a whole. (In PPP conversion US $1= ₹15.11.)

Compared to the poverty lines based on the methodology of the Expert Group (Tendulkar), the poverty lines estimated by the Expert Group (Rangarajan) are 19 per cent and 41 per cent higher in rural and urban areas, respectively. The Expert Group (Rangarajan) uses the Modified Mixed Recall Period consumption expenditure data of the NSSO as these are considered to be more precise compared to the MRP, which was used by the Expert Group (Tendulkar) and the URP, which was used by earlier estimations. 67 per cent of the increase in the rural poverty line and 28 per cent of the increase in the urban poverty line is because of the shift from MRP to MMRP.

The national level poverty lines are disaggregated into state-specific poverty lines in order to reflect the inter-state price differential. The method of constructing the state-wise poverty lines from the national level poverty line in 2011-12 is broadly similar to that outlined by the Expert Group (Tendulkar). Implicit prices are calculated from the quantity and value of consumption gathered in NSS consumer expenditure data of the 68th Round (2011-12). From these, state relative to all-India Fisher price index has been computed, separately in rural and urban areas. Using the Fisher Index, the inter-state price differential is calculated separately in rural and urban areas and from these the national poverty lines (separately in rural and urban areas) in 2011-12 are disaggregated into state-specific poverty lines.

Using these and the state-specific distribution of persons by expenditure groups (NSS), state-specific ratios of rural and urban poverty were estimated. State-level poverty ratio was estimated as weighted average of the rural and urban poverty ratios and the national poverty ratio was computed again as the population-weighted average of state-wise poverty ratios.

The Expert Group (Rangarajan) estimates that the 30.9 per cent of the rural population and 26.4 per cent of the urban population was below the poverty line in 2011-12. The all-India ratio was 29.5 per cent. In rural India, 260.5 million individuals were below poverty and in urban India 102.5 million were under poverty. Totally, 363 million were below poverty in 2011-12. The state-specific poverty ratio and number of poor estimated for the year 2011-12 is given in the expert group (Rangarajan) report (GoI, 2014)

Expert Group (Rangarajan) also estimated poverty ratios for the year 2009-10. The price inflation during the period 2009-10 to 2011-12, at the state level (separately in rural and urban areas), has been calculated from the increase in the cost of the consumption basket of the poor, that is the poverty line as estimated by the

Planning Commission for these two years using the Expert Group (Tendulkar) methodology.

The estimate of poverty ratio for the years 2009-10 and 2011-12 derived from the Expert Group (Rangarajan) methodology and Tendulkar methodology are summarised in Table 1.2.

Table 1.2

Poverty Estimates in 2009-10 and 2011-12

Year	*Poverty Ratio*			*No. of Poor (million)*		
	Rural	*Urban*	*Total*	*Rural*	*Urban*	*Total*
			Expert Group (Rangarajan)			
2009-10	39.6	35.1	38.2	325.9	128.7	454.6
2011-12	30.9	26.4	29.5	260.5	102.5	363.0
Reduction (percentage points)	8.7	8.7	8.7	65.4	26.2	91.6
			Expert Group (Tendulkar)			
2009-10	33.8	20.9	29.8	278.2	76.5	354.7
2011-12	25.7	13.7	21.9	216.7	53.1	269.8
Reduction (percentage points)	8.1	7.2	7.9	61.5	23.4	84.9

Source: GoI (2014).

A comparison of the poverty ratio for the two years 2009-10 and 2011-12 derived from the Expert Group (Rangarajan) method and the Expert Group (Tendulkar) method shows that the average level of poverty ratio derived from the Expert Group (Rangarajan) method is higher than that derived from the Expert Group (Tendulkar) method. The all-India poverty ratio derived from the Expert Group (Rangarajan) method is 8.4 percentage points higher in 2009-10 and 7.6 percentage points higher in 2011-12 than that derived by the Planning Commission using the Expert Group (Tendulkar) method. The all-India poverty ratio in Expert Group (Rangarajan) fell from 38.2 per cent to 29.5 per cent. Totally, 91.6 million individuals were lifted out of poverty during this period. Though Rangarajan Committee methodology gives higher level of absolute poverty ratio, the reduction in poverty ratio from Rangarajan method is not very different than that of Tendulkar method.

The Expert Group (Rangarajan) recommends the updation of the poverty line in the future using the Fisher Index. The weighting diagram for this effort can be drawn from the NSSO's Consumer Expenditure Survey. For the food group, it recommends that the current practice of relying on the unit values derivable from the NSSO consumer expenditure surveys should continue till such time a new CPI (consumer price index) of CSO with a weighting diagram based on the 2011-12 pattern of consumption becomes available. In respect of non-food items, the price indices available in the existing CSO Consumer Price Indices can be used in the construction of requisite Fisher indices. Once the new series of CPI numbers (with 2011-12 as the base year) becomes available, it may be used for updating the future poverty line.

Clarifications on the Issues Raised by Others

Since the submission of the report of Expert Group (Rangarajan), there have been few comments on the report published particularly in The *Economic and Political Weekly* (Ray and Sinha, 2014; Mishra, 2014; Subramanian, 2014) and *The Hindu* Newspaper (Deaton and Dreze, 2014). Of course they also indicated the positive aspects of the report. We provide clarifications below on various issues raised by them.

What is New in the Approach for Poverty Line?

It may be noted that poverty line computed by Rangarajan group has three components: (a) food component, (b) normative level of expenditure for essential non-food items such as education, clothing, conveyence and house rent, and (c) behaviourally determined expenditure for other non-food items. The Group has gone back to the idea of separate poverty line baskets for rural and urban areas. This stands to reason. This is also consistent with the way we have derived the poverty line. The introduction of norms for certain kinds of non-food expenditures is an innovation. It is a simple recognition of the fact that these expenditures constituted a significant part of total consumption. In the absence of any other normative criteria, the median fractile class expenditures were treated as the norm. In fact, non-food consumption as a proportion of total consumption has been steadily rising. That is why the Group decided to take a fresh look at the basket rather than only updating the old basket for price changes.

Mishra (2014) says that the expert group takes commodity basket from two fractile groups and it poses a behavioural dilemma. It may be noted that when we adopt two norms one for food and the other for certain non-food expenditures, obviously the emerging basket will not correspond to the behavioural pattern of a particular expenditure class. Our attempt has been to estimate the level of private consumption expenditure which will meet certain minimum requirements.

Srinivasan (2007) calls for a new approach to poverty measurement. He says that, "Useful starting points for a new approach lie in anchoring poverty lines in social norms and in the distinction made by PPD[8] between goods and services to be bought by households from their own resources and those to be supplied by the state, thus providing a meaningful way of distinguishing the responsibilities of households (i.e., the private sphere) and those of the state (i.e., the public sphere)." In a personal correspondence with one of the authors of this paper he elaborates his idea as follows.

> I have suggested an alternative, namely to start from a socially defined poverty bundle of goods and define as those who do not consume that bundle. In valuing the bundle and updating it requires the use of prices actually paid by the poor and also excluding that part of the bundle whose cost is in part met by subsidies.

The suggestion of Srinivasan that we should start from a 'socially defined poverty bundle of goods', is a good idea. But, the problem is how to arrive at such a socially defined poverty bundle. In some ways, this is precisely what we have done regarding private expenditure. We have arrived at a minimum level of private consumption expenditure both in relation to food and non-food items. Unless, a method is

8. PPD refers to Perspective Planning Division of the Planning Commission

specified to arrive at socially defined poverty bundle of goods, it may be difficult to measure poverty. We have discussed below on the contribution of public expenditures.

Among other things, Subramanian (2014) provides a critique of the expert group's methodology for identifying the poverty line particularly unvarying "poverty line basket". It may be noted that the report of the expert group chaired by Lakdawala discussed the issues of fixed commodity basket and varying commodity basket and opted for the fixed one for comparability. It may, however, be noted that while the basket may remain the same in terms of composition, weights for price indices could change since the updation of the poverty line is to be done using the Fisher Index. As the Expert Group (Tendulkar) says, "the proposed price indices (Fisher Ideal indices in technical terms) incorporate both the observed all-India and the state level consumption patterns in the weighting structure of the price indices" (GoI, 2009: 2).

Use of Calories

Deaton and Drèze (2014) criticise the group for going back to calorie norms. Ray and Sinha (2014) appreciate the use of calories but they do not agree with sharp reduction in rural daily calorie requirements. They also mention Amrtya Sen who said that there was no decline of calories for the population around the poverty line. Apart from taking the recent ICMR norms, the revised calorie norm is also justified on the following grounds:

i. First, as a recent study by Meenakshi and Viswanathan (2013) shows, the average calorie norms could be significantly lower if we replace the 95th percentile heights and a BMI of 21 that underline the ICMR norms for adults by a possibly more appropriate (for the current adult population whose height is given) median (or mean) heights and a BMI of 19 that is still higher than the lower limit of 18.5 that defines a healthy adult.
ii. Secondly, we have the idea (Sukhatme, 1981) of a margin of homeostatic adaptation within which individuals can adapt,

without adverse impact on health and activity status, to variation in intakes around the norms.

These two factors would suggest that the calorie norms be treated as lying in range of say, ±10 per cent, where intakes at the lower level need not compromise an adult's health and activity status.

The new poverty line is not limited only to calorie intake but also extends to fats and proteins. As mentioned above, calories, fats and proteins are used mainly for locating food component. It is true that there is no direct correlation between calorie and nutrition. Some use calorie norm directly as cut off for measuring poverty. This method may give implausible results (see Dev, 2005). There are many other factors which contribute to nutrition. But taken in conjunction with other factors mentioned in the Report, relating minimum food consumption to calorie, fat and protein requirements appears to be a reasonable approach. The Expert Group (Rangarajan) takes the considered position that, taken in conjunction with public provisioning of a range of public goods and services (sanitation, drinking water, immunisation and vaccination etc.) on a universal basis, the access to the food component of the PLB will have a favourable impact on the nutrition-status outcomes for the population. Without such norms, the minimum level may turn out to be arbitrary. Tendulkar Group itself did not abandon calorie norms. They took the urban poverty basket as given. They also claimed that ultimately the poverty line they recommended satisfied FAO norms.

Ray and Sinha (2014) rightly points out the importance of micronutrients for nutrition. We recognise the need for micronutrients but data on this are not readily available to include it in the food component of poverty line. They also mention that variations in dietary habits vary across regions and poverty line should be based on state variations in consumption. This is not a new thing and these issues were discussed in Lakdawala expert group report. In fact, there was a note of dissent by S. Guhan highlighting the need for separate poverty lines based on variation in consumption of different states. But, all the expert groups (Lakdawala and subsequent reports) decided to have all India consumption basket only.

Non-Food Criteria

One of the novel features of the Rangarajan Committee Report is that for the first time it incorporates a normative component for four essentials of non-food items. The Committee recommended that the observed expenditures on these four items by households located in the median fractile (45-50 fractile) be treated as the normative minimum private consumption expenditure on these items. Some observers have commented that both selection of items as essentials and locating households in the median fractile are arbitrary. It may be noted that the Committee had to use some judgement in selecting items and fractile group. One can use different judgement and change the items to be included in normative component and also locate different fractile groups. Any normative criterion can be subject to such a criticism of arbitrariness.

Multi-dimensional Poverty

Ray and Sinha (2014) are critical of the report saying that the group did not widen the concept of poverty in terms of multidimensional poverty as mentioned in the terms of reference. They use NSS and NFHS data to highlight multidimensionality. Subramanian (2014) also says that the expert group has "forfeited an opportunity to press the case for a multidimensional assessment of poverty". It may be noted that the group discussed these issues and has given the reasons in the report why it has not attempted estimating multidimensional poverty. The search for non-income dimensions of poverty possibly stems from a view that, in terms of the capabilities approach to the concept and measurement of poverty, some of these 'capabilities', may not be tightly linked to the privately purchased consumption basket in terms of which the poverty lines are currently drawn. Therefore, poverty based on income or consumption is different from deprivations based on education or health

Oxford Poverty and Human Development Initiatives (OPHI) and UNDP together developed MPI (multidimensional poverty index). It used 10 indicators relating to health, education and standard of living. However, these multidimensional indicators/measures raise several issues regarding their measurability, aggregation across indicators, and, crucially, of data bases that provide the requisite information at reasonably short intervals. These need to be considered and evaluated carefully. For example, child mortality indicator has a problem as it is for population groups and not for households.

Aggregation is another problem. In principle, they should be independent. Access to safe drinking water, for example, cannot be aggregated with indicators, of, say, child mortality. Even in respect of independent indicators, analytically appropriate rules of aggregation require that all of them relate to the same household. It is this factor that dictated the choice of NFHS-3 (2005-06) as the data base for OPHDI-study, which, in turn, dictated the choice of the indicators used in the study. The 2005-06 Index would hardly be appropriate for the present day. More generally, this requirement poses several data constraints. For example, Decennial Censuses provide valuable information on access of households to a range of housing amenities—water, electricity—and about the materials used for the floor, the walls and the roof of structures that house the population. Besides the obvious issues of periodicity (once in 10 years), this information cannot be combined with those from NSS surveys on social consumption (on access to publicly provided good and services) or the NSS Employment-Unemployment Surveys that capture school attendance of children and educational outcome for all. It is also difficult to combine NSS data on consumption poverty with other deprivations which relate to some other households.

Most importantly, the data derived from sources listed above (the same holds good for the data collected under the Socio Economic Caste Census (SECC) 2011 as well) cannot be combined with the Consumer Expenditure Surveys—the data base for poverty line defined in terms of consumption basket as they relate to different sets of households. This also rules out combining the data with indicators based on "other Criteria" as proposed in the TOR.

It may be noted that the group is not against multidimensional poverty or deprivations. One can analyse the progress of non-income indicators like education, health, sanitation, drinking water, child mortality etc., over time along with income or consumption poverty. But, aggregating all of them into an index would have several problems as indicated above. Deaton and Dreze (2014) also indicate that "it is important to supplement expenditure-based poverty estimates with other indicators of living standards, relating for instance to nutrition, health, education and the quality of the environment".

On multidimensional issues Srinivasan (2007) says viewing the public services as another dimension besides consumption in a multidimensional conceptualisation of poverty is more fruitful. However, he is critical of multidimensional indices. He says that "collapsing many relevant but not necessarily commensurate dimensions into a single index defined as an arbitrarily weighted sum of disparate indexes makes little sense. The Hurman Development Index pioneered by the United Nations Development Programme is an example of an arbitrarily weighted sum of non-commensurate indexes. It certainly is not a multidimensional conceptualisation in any meaningful sense but simply yet another arbitrary unidimensional index" (Srinivasan, 2007: 4162).

In the minds of most people, being rich or poor is associated with levels of income. The various non-income indicators of poverty are in fact reflections of inadequate income. Defining poverty in terms of income or in the absence of such data in terms of expenditure seems most appropriate and it is this method which is followed in most countries.

Higher Urban Poverty in Many States

Deaton and Dreze (2014) and EPW (2014) say that in Rangarajan group method urban poverty ratio is higher than rural poverty in many states. Based on Tendulkar expert group methodology, urban poverty is lower than rural poverty (except for Punjab) in 2011-2012. In fact, there was severe criticism of Tendulkar expert group methodology for urban basket for rural areas and underestimating urban poverty. Their report has also been criticised for not taking into account the aspirations of people. Therefore, Rangarajan group tried to correct this problem by including median fractile expenditures for four essential non-food items.

It is true that based on Ragarajan expert group methodology, 13 out of 28 states showed higher urban poverty than rural poverty. These states are: Andhra Pradesh, Bihar, Goa, Haryana, Jammu & Kashmir, Karnataka, Kerala, Manipur, Nagaland, Punjab, Rajastan, Tripura, Uttar Pradesh and Uttarakhand.

What are the possible explanations for higher urban poverty in some states? One can give the following explanations.

It may be noted that Lakdawala committee based estimates for 2004-05 show that 10 out of 28 states showed higher urban poverty than rural poverty. Lakdawala group and Rangarajan group have consumption baskets separately for rural and urban areas. On the other hand, Tendulkar group had only one consumption basket for urban areas which is used for rural areas. Obviously, in Tendulkar group methodology, rural poverty would be higher than urban poverty because getting urban basket in rural areas is costly. In contrast, there are two baskets (rural and urban baskets) separately in Lakdwala group and Tendulkar group.

In Rangarajan group, the median fractile (45-50%) values of clothing expenses, rent, conveyance and education expenses are treated as the normative requirements of the basic non-food expenses of clothing, housing, mobility and education of a poverty line basket. This works out to ₹141 per capita per month in rural areas and ₹407 in urban areas. The basic non-food expenses constitute 14.5 per cent of total poverty line in rural areas and 29.1 per cent in urban areas. It shows that the share of these items in urban areas is twice to that of rural areas. It is known that particularly house rents and conveyance charges are much higher in urban areas than rural areas. As a result of this higher share of basic non-foods, the share of total non-foods in total poverty line in urban areas is 53 per cent as compared to 43 per cent in rural areas.

One may ask the question: why only 13 states have higher urban poverty? What about other 15 states which have higher rural poverty than urban poverty? It is possible in these 15 states, in spite of inclusion of normative expenses on basic non-foods and higher expenses on housing and conveyance, the purchasing power of more number of people in rural areas are not matching with those of urban population. This needs a detailed study.

It is also possible that in spite of MGNREGA and other schemes, significant number of rural poor may be migrating to urban areas in search of employment. In other words, poverty is being exported from rural areas to urban areas. Studies have shown that seasonal migration is quite high from rural to urban areas. This also needs investigation.

NAS-NSS Consumption Differences

Ray and Sinha (2014) say that the committee discussed NAS-NSS differences but lost opportunity in suggesting a compromise to resolve the issue. It may be noted that these two estimates of consumption (NAS and household survey based) do not match in any country and India is no exception. What is alarming in India is that the difference between NAS and NSS is widening over time. For example, the difference was less than 10 per cent in the late 1970s; it rose to 50 per cent in 2009-10. The differences are much higher for non-food (46%) as compared to food. Some adjustments made in the report reduced the differences from 45.8 per cent to 32.5 per cent. But still the differences are high. Apart from problems in NAS, the fatigue of the respondents in NSS might not be able to capture some of the non-food items. This can be rectified in future NSS. However, still it is difficult to reconcile the differences between NAS and NSS particularly for non-food items.

Poverty Measures in Other Countries

There are also comments that we should look at the poverty measures of other countries. The expert group looked at the methodology of poverty estimation of other countries. Most of the developing countries use consumption basket poverty line. Developed countries generally use the concept of relative poverty. In some countries, poverty line is exogenously set proportion of mean or median income of population. Ray and Sinha (2014) also talk about inequality and relative poverty. However, if we look at the Indian data the proportion of population with consumption as a fraction of the median remains largely invariant over time.

Reviewing the method of estimation of poverty in other countries and World Bank, the Rangarajan expert group arrived at the conclusion that neither their methodological nor procedural aspects are superior to what is being used in India at present. The estimates of poverty in India are based on a methodology which stands far apart for it is able to measure the incidence of poverty by capturing the demographic pattern and consumer behaviour separately in rural and urban areas and also by capturing the state-wise variation in the prices of goods and services.

Public Expenditure and Poverty

Poverty line is based on private consumer expenditure. If we take into account public expenditure, the actual well being of the household will be higher than what is indicated by the poverty line. In the seven-year period 2004-05 to 2011-12, public expenditures on education and health per capita at constant 2004-05 prices have nearly doubled with an implied CAGR (compound annual growth rate) of close to 10 per cent per annum. Given that these services are, typically, provided at heavily subsidised prices—if not given free, the reported private expenditures as captured in the NSS Consumer Expenditure Surveys on them would be lower than their true value. However, in the absence of data on the distribution of the public expenditures on these social services by size-class of private consumption expenditure, they can-not be factored into either the construction of the poverty line or in the assessment of their impact on measured poverty. In the case of of PDS (public distribution system), we do have information on the MPCE of households using PDS and the quantities of grains etc. bought. One could, therefore, analyse the impact of PDS on measured poverty (Himanshu and Sen, 2013).

Poverty Ratio for Eligibility Under Programmes

Finally, the Planning Commission has earlier decided to delink the consumption based poverty estimates for allocating resources to states. The Expert Group deliberated on the issue of use of poverty ratio for determining the eligibility and entitlements for a wide range of poverty alleviation programmes and social welfare schemes implemented by various Ministries and Departments of the GoI in association with the State governments.

The Group recommends that the beneficiaries under target group oriented schemes of the Government may be selected from the deprivation-specific ranking of households. Such ranking of households could be generated for a large number of indicators representing deprivation and levels of living for which the information has been gathered at the household and individual level in the SECC-2011 and population census. The beneficiaries could be selected from this set of households until the resources earmarked for the programme/scheme permit. Ray and Sinha (2014) also argue for multidimensional measures for identification of the poor. Poverty ratio of Planning Commission can play an important role in deciding allocation of resources among States although now it is delinked as mentioned above. The Ministries and Departments in association with the State governments may draw the guidelines for defining the beneficiaries for their programmes. The process could be similar in rural and urban areas.

Conclusion

To conclude, one has to review from time to time the methodologies for arriving poverty estimates in keeping with the changing needs of the population. Poverty lines are only approximations to the socially accepted minimum standards. Thus, in any poverty line approach, an inevitable element of arbitrariness is inescapable. It is by nature subjective and judgmental. There is a hilarious description of how the poverty line evolved in the United States in the latest book by Deaton (2013) entitled *The Great Escape*. Nevertheless an attempt has been made in the report of Expert Group (Rangarajan) to approach the subject on methodology of measurement of poverty as systematically as possible.

The methodology adopted by the new group on poverty is based on sound principles. However, as the group has clearly indicated, this measure is not considered as an appropriate basis for determining entitlements under various programmes. Each programme focusing on a particular deprivation may have to choose that criterion which is most appropriate for it. But to obtain a general picture of the progress of the country, a suitable measure on poverty is useful. Poverty is not the same as hunger. Hunger is far worse. Nor does the poverty line means a comfortable standard of living. It represents absolute minimum. Obviously, policy should work towards not only to reduce the number of people below that line but also ensure that people in general enjoy a much higher standard of living. Numbers do indicate that poverty ratio in India is coming down even though it may remain at a high level. Policy makers must continue to follow the two-fold strategy of letting the economy grow fast and attacking poverty directly through poverty alleviation programmes.

References

Deaton, Angus (2013). *Great Escape: Health, Wealth and the Origins of Inequality*. USA: Princeton University Press.

Deaton, A. and J. Dreze (2014). "Squaring the Poverty Circle", *The Hindu*, 25 July.

Dev, S. Mahendra (2005). "Calorie Norms and Poverty", *Economic and Political Weekly* 40(8).

EPW (2014). "Rangarajan's Measure of Poverty", Editorial, *Economic and Political Weekly* 31, 2 August.

GoI (1979). *Report of the Task Force on Projection of Minimum Needs and Effective Consumption Demands.* Chaired by Y.K. Alagh. Planning Commission, Government of India.

———. (1993). *Report of the Expert Group on Estimation of Proportion and Number of Poor.* Chaired by D.T. Lakdawala. Planning Commission, Government of India.

———. (2009). *Report of the Expert Group to Review the Methodology for Estimation of Poverty.* Chaired by S.D. Tendulkar. Planning Commission, Government of India.

———. (2014).*Report of the Expert Group to Review the Methodology for Measurement of Poverty.* Chaired by C. Rangarajan. Planning Commission, Government of India.

Himanshu and Abhijit Sen (2013). "In-kind Transfers: Impact on Poverty", *Economic and Political Weekly* 48(45-46).

Meenakshi, J.V. and Brinda Viswanathan (2013). "Estimation of Calorie Norms and Measurement of Food Intake: Some Implications for the Magnitudes of the Prevalence of Undernutrition in India", *Indian Economic Review* (Special Issue on "Perspectives on Economic Development and Policy) XLVIII: 167-88.

Mishra, Srijit (2014). "Reading between the Poverty Line", *Economic and Political Weekly* 49(39), 27 September.

Ray, Ranjan and Kompal Sinha (2014). "Rangarajan Committee Report on Poverty Measurement: Another Lost Opportunity", *Economic and Political Weekly* 49(32), 9 August.

Subramanian, S. (2014). "The Poverty Line, Getting It Wong Again ...and Again", *Economic and Political Weekly* 49(2).

Srinivasan, T.N. (2007). "Poverty Lines in India: Reflections after the Patna Conference", *Economic and Political Weekly* 429(41): 4155-65, 13 October.

———. (2013). "Planning, Poverty and Political Economy of Reforms: A Tribute to Suresh Tendulkar", *Indian Economic Review* (Special Issue on "Perspectives on Economic Development and Policy) 48: 1-32.

Sukhatme, P.V. (1981). "On Measurement of Poverty", *Economic and Political Weekly* 16(32): 1318-24.

World Bank (2014). *2011 International Comparison Program Results.* Washington D.C. *http://icp.worldbank.org/*

The Expert Group Report (Rangarajan) is based on contributions of all the members of the group. Besides the authors, the group included Dr K. Sundaram, Mr Mahesh Vyas and Mr K.L. Datta. We thank all of them as well as Dr Savita Sharma and her colleagues in Planning Commission. Usual disclaimers apply.

2

NSS and SECC

Measurement of Poverty and Deprivation

Recently, government has released the Socio-Economic Caste Census (SECC) 2011 data. There have been views in the media that hereafter we need not have consumption based poverty estimates using National Sample Surveys (NSS) data. It is viewed that SECC data would alone be enough to estimate poverty and deprivation. The purpose of this article is to briefly examine the differences between the two and clarify that NSS consumption based poverty estimates are still relevant. SECC based estimates are important, but it does not substitutes for NSS based poverty ratios.

Measurement of Poverty Based on NSS Estimates

In India, we have had a long history of studies on measurement of poverty. The methodology for estimation of poverty used by the erstwhile Planning Commission has been based on the recommendations made by various Expert Groups. In June 2012, the Government of India appointed an Expert Group (C. Rangarajan as Chairman) to take a fresh look at the methodology for the measurement of poverty.

The Expert Group (Rangarajan) has gone back to the idea of separate poverty line baskets for rural and urban areas unlike the Tendulkar Committee which took urban poverty as given and used it as the common basket for rural and urban households. In defining the consumption basket separating the poor from the rest, the new Expert Group took the view that it should contain a food component that satisfied certain minimum nutrition requirements as well as some normative level of consumption expenditure for essential non-food item groups (education, clothing, conveyance and house rent) besides a residual set of behaviourally determined non-food expenditure. The introduction of norms for certain kinds of non-food expenditures is an innovation. In the absence of any other normative criteria, the median fractile class expenditures were treated as the norm.

Based on the analysis presented in the Expert Group Report, MPCE (monthly per capita consumption expenditure) of ₹972 in rural areas and ₹1,407 in urban areas is treated as the poverty line at the all India level. Assuming five members for a family, this will imply a monthly per household expenditure of ₹4,860 in rural areas and ₹7,035 in urban areas. The Expert Group estimates that the 30.9 per cent of the rural population and 26.4 per cent of the urban population was below the poverty line in 2011-12. The all-India ratio was 29.5 per cent.

The estimates of poverty provide the proportion and size of the poor population and their spread across states and broad regions. But, they can't be used for identification of the individual poor which is necessary to ensure that the benefits of these programmes and schemes reach only the deserved and the target group.

SECC, Deprivation and Identification of the Poor

After the release of SECC estimates, some commented that earlier targeted programmes were designed based on sample surveys and SECC was an innovation for the first time. This is not true. Even previously for identification of poor, BPL (below poverty line) censuses were conducted. The first two BPL censuses (conducted in 1992 and 1997) yielded the estimate of percentage and number of poor households at village, block, district and state level, and the beneficiaries in these programmes were chosen by the State governments depending upon their location/position in the BPL list. The third BPL Census was conducted in 2002. It did not identify the number of poor households straightaway or estimate their numbers as in the previous two Censuses. Instead, it ranked the households within the village in terms of their socio-economic status, based on 13 indicators reflecting the levels of living and quality of life. SECC

2011 is thus part of this continuing process of conducting BPL Censuses in rural areas.

According to SECC data 8.69 crore out of 17.91 all rural households have one of the 7 deprivations. In other words, 48.5 per cent of all rural households suffer from at least on 1 of 7 deprivations. 30 per cent of households suffer from 2 deprivations, while 13 per cent have 3 deprivations. Only 0.01 per cent households suffer from all deprivations. The automatically included contributed 0.92 per cent of the total rural households. Information on urban households are not yet available.

The rural poverty ratio estimated by the expert group based on NSS data was around 30.9 per cent in 2011-12. This is almost equal to households with two deprivations plus automatically included. However, NSS based estimates are per capita based while SECC data refer to households. A look at 7 deprivations shows that they are not deprivations in the conventional sense of deprived of income, health and education etc. Therefore, the question is whether SECC data is appropriate to estimate poverty ratios. For example, it is true that landless households deriving a major part of their income from manual labour constitute the largest number under deprivation households. It is not clear whether landlessness (or manual labour) can be sufficient to conclude that they are suffering from poverty. Over time landlessness will increase and people will diversify their income with rise in non-agricultural activities and migration. In the same way, some of the other criteria are not clear indicators of poverty.

Lastly, what is the rationale for having poverty estimates based on consumption estimates?

First, in the minds of most people, being rich or poor is associated with levels of income. The various non-income indicators of poverty are in fact reflections of inadequate income. Defining poverty in terms of income or in the absence of such data in terms of expenditure seems more appropriate and it is this method which is followed in most countries for measurement of poverty.

Second, historically, the number of identified poor based on the successive BPL Censuses in rural areas has differed widely from the measured poverty. For example, the percentage of households identified as poor in the first BPL Census in 1992 was nearly twice the poverty ratio estimated by the Planning Commission. Usually the identified poor households through these Censuses contain a mix of poor and non-poor for which there could be several reasons. One of the main reasons behind such mix-up could be due to the fact that people know beforehand that the Census was going to decide the status of the household as poor or non-poor and therefore its entitlement.

Third, the deprivation criteria by themselves do not indicate the level of poverty. A judgement has to be made as to the number of deprivations taken together constitute a measure of poverty. This can turn out to be highly subjective.

What is the purpose of NSS consumption based estimates if they are not used for allocation of funds and capping beneficiaries under government programmes? These poverty ratios would be used basically for assessing the changes in poverty at national and state levels or district level. This will be useful for making appropriate policies. For example, one can examine changes in poverty in different phases of post-reform period to understand what impact anti-poverty programmes in conjunction with growth have had on poverty.

To conclude, SECC and NSS data based estimates have different purposes. SECC would be important for identification of beneficiaries of programmes while NSS based estimates would be useful to assess changes in levels of living at the macro level over time.

3

Public Expenditure on Social Services and Impact on Poverty

The official poverty ratios in India are estimated using certain minimum level of private consumer expenditure on food and non-food items. For example, according to Rangarajan Committee Report on Poverty, the MPCE (monthly per capita consumption expenditure) of ₹972 in rural areas and ₹1,407 in urban areas is treated as the poverty line at the all India level in 2011-12. This level of private expenditure has to be seen in the context of public expenditure that is being incurred in areas like health, education, food security, sanitation, and drinking water. In this article we argue that the actual well-being of the household will be higher than what is indicated by the poverty line, if we take into account public expenditure along with private expenditure. This aspect is specifically dealt with by the Rangarajan Committee.

The issue of public expenditure on social sector has been mentioned in earlier committees on poverty as well. For example, the 1962 expert group of the Perspective Planning Division (PPD) of the Planning Commission recommended a national minimum of private consumption expenditure on food and non-food items for estimating poverty ratios. The Committee Report says that "this national minimum excludes expenditure on health and education, both of which are expected to be provided by the State according to the Constitution and in the light of its other commitments".

Similarly, Lakdawala Committee on Poverty (1993) says that the "poverty line derived from personal consumption patterns and levels do not take into account items of social consumption such as basic education and health, drinking water supply, sanitation, environmental standards etc., in terms of normative requirements or effective access". It also says "consumption of free goods and services provided by the State or charitable institutions is not recorded. Social consumption of these publicly provided services is in the nature of transfer from the government to the people. In other words, the real levels of living of the poor, inclusive of social consumption are expected to be higher than what is reflected through the estimates of private consumption expenditure reported in NSS data".

Public expenditure, particularly in the areas of health, education, food, sanitation etc., constitutes a significant proportion of the total consumer expenditure of these items. Their proportion is high particularly among the poor as these services are provided either free or at nominal cost to them. In the seven-year period 2004-05 to 2011-12, public expenditures on education and health per capita at constant 2004-05 prices have nearly doubled with an implied compound annual growth rate of close to 10 per cent per annum (Table 3.1).

Table 3.1

Per Capita Per Month Public Expenditure at Constant Prices (2004-05)

Year	*Education*	*Health*
2004-05	78	20
2005-06	90	25
2006-07	85	26
2007-08	95	27
2008-09	101	28
2009-10	129	32
2010-11	146	36
2011-12	157	38

Source: Estimated from Budget documents, Ministry of Finance, GoI.

Given that these services are, typically, provided at heavily subsidised prices—if not given free, the reported private expenditures as captured in the NSS Consumer Expenditure Surveys on them would be lower than their true value. However, in the absence of data on the distribution of the public expenditures on these social services by size-class of private consumption expenditure, they cannot be factored into either the construction of the poverty line or in the assessment of their impact on measured poverty. However, it is reasonable to assume that the bulk of the public expenditures on health and education would have gone to meet the needs of lower deciles of population.

Unlike in education and health, in the case of PDS (public distribution system), we do have information on the MPCE of households using PDS and the quantities of grains etc. bought. One could, therefore, analyse the impact of PDS on measured poverty. Himanshu and Sen (2013)[1] estimate the size of PDS transfers and the impact of these transfers on poverty. According to their estimates, the value of PDS transfer was 2.4 per cent of MPCE for the population as a whole and 5.2 per cent of MPCE for the bottom 40 per cent. In other words, poor benefited more than others due to these in-kind food transfers. Their study also shows that with PDS transfers, total poverty ratio (Tendulkar methodology) was 30.68 per cent in 2009-10. Without PDS transfers, poverty ratio was higher at 33.85 per cent in the same year.

A survey on "Social Consumption: Education" was conducted in NSS 71st round (January-June 2014). In this survey, information was obtained for each student on various educational incentives received by them such as free education or tuition fee waived, scholarship/stipend/reimbursement, books or stationery free or at a subsidised price, mid-day meal, student's concession in public transport etc.

Table 3.2 provides proportion of students receiving scholarships in rural and urban areas for each quintile class of MPCE. Percentage of students receiving scholarships was higher for lower quintile classes. For example, in rural areas, 33 per cent of students received scholarships for bottom quintile while compared to that of 13 per cent for highest quintile. The table also shows that female students were getting more scholarships than males

1. Himanshu and Abhijit Sen (2013). "In-kind Transfers: Impact on Poverty", *Economic and Political Weekly* 48(45-46).

Table 3.2

Percentage of Students Receiving Scholarship for Each Quintile Class of UMPCE: 2014

Quintile Classes of UMPCE	*Rural*			*Urban*		
	Male	*Female*	*Person*	*Male*	*Female*	*Person*
1	30.7	36.0	33.2	16.0	20.1	18.0
2	26.4	29.9	28.1	11.4	14.0	12.6
3	22.5	24.4	23.3	9.7	11.8	10.7
4	19.0	24.0	21.2	7.6	8.5	8.0
5	11.9	14.8	13.1	5.6	5.5	5.6
All	21.9	26.1	23.8	10.0	12.2	11.0

Note: UMPCE: Usual monthly per capita expenditure.

Source: NSS 71st Round (January-June, 2014). Report no.575.

The survey on education also shows that around 57 per cent of males and 63 per cent of female students were getting free education in primary schools. In the case of upper primary, these percentages were 58 per cent for males and 64 per cent for females. Regarding secondary schools, 32 per cent of males and 37 per cent of females were getting free education. The proportion of students getting free education must be much higher for the poor. Similarly, poor must be getting higher benefits from the public expenditure on health.

To conclude, it is suggested here that increased public expenditure on health, education and other social services will have to be taken into account while assessing the trends in poverty. This is because the actual well being is higher than what is indicated by the poverty line and it has policy implications.

4

Poverty Estimation

Headcount and Depth

Recent World Bank (2015)[1] report on poverty brings out poverty ratios across countries including India. According to these estimates, India's poverty ratio based on 'uniform reference period' (URP) in which recall period in the sample survey was 30 days for all items was 21.2 per cent in 2011-12. The poverty line is $1.90 per capita per day. The Report says that poverty in India could be even lower at 12.4 per cent if we use 'modified mixed reference period' (MMRP) in which there are three recall periods depending on the nature of items.

Differing Estimates

The Rangarajan Committee on poverty estimates that 29.5 per cent of India's population was BPL (below poverty line) in 2011-12. The poverty line for all India is around ₹1,105 per capita per month. In terms of latest PPP (purchasing power parity) terms this comes to around $2.44 per capita per day. The World Bank's poverty line of $1.90 per capita per day is about 78 per cent of Rangarajan's committee's poverty line. Thus, the lower poverty line was the reason for the lower poverty ratio of 12.4 per cent in World Bank estimates.

World Bank report also talks about depth of poverty in terms of person-equivalent headcounts. According to the Report, the depth elasticity at the global level between 1990 and 2012 was 1.18 indicating that the reductions in traditional HCRs (head count ratios) were accompanied by even-larger reductions in person-equivalent

---

1. World Bank (2015). *Ending Poverty and Sharing Prosperity*. Washington DC.

poverty ratios. This is true in the regions such as South Asia where bulk of the poor reside.

Depth of Poverty

We examine here the depth of poverty for India in a different way by looking at the poverty ratios using different cut-offs of PL (poverty line). The first issue is whether the poverty ratios with lowered PL cut-offs are declining as fast as those with PL or the raised PL cut-offs. The second one is about the location of the poor i.e., whether the poor are located much below the PL or around the PL.

One conclusion is that even if we raise the PL to 125 per cent, the reduction in poverty ratio was 9 percentage points between 2009-10 and 2011-12 (Table 4.1). This is also true for poverty ratio based on 115 per cent of PL. In the case of 85 per cent and 75 per cent of PLs, the percentage points decline was lower than those of raised PL. But, if we adjust for base poverty ratio, the decline of poverty ratio was faster for 85 per cent and 75 per cent PLs compared to those of 100 per cent to 125 per cent PLs.

Table 4.1

Poverty Ratios using Different Cut-offs: Rural and Urban Areas, All India

Poverty Line Cut-offs	*Rural*		*Urban*		*Total*	
	2009-10	*2011-12*	*2009-10*	*2011-12*	*2009-10*	*2011-12*
125% of PL	60.0	51.3	49.8	40.1	57.1	48.1
115% of PL	53.0	43.5	44.0	34.7	50.4	41.0
100% of PL	39.6	30.9	35.2	26.8	38.2	29.5
85% of PL	25.6	18.3	25.4	18.1	25.5	18.3
75% of PL	16.7	11.1	18.5	12.4	17.2	11.5
50% of PL	2.0	1.4	4.4	2.2	2.7	1.7

Note: 100% refers to Rangarajan committee's poverty line.

Source: NSS Household Level data.

HCR is criticised on the ground that it does not measure the 'depth' of poverty. It is seen, however, that more than 50 per cent of the poor lies between 75 per cent of the PL and the PL. This is true both in 2009-10 and 2011-12. In fact, 65 per cent of rural poor and 61 per cent total poor lie between 75 per cent of PL and PL in 2011-

2012. It may also be noted that many of the non-poor also live just above the PL between 115 per cent of PL and PL or between 125 per cent of PL and PL. Another point is that there is negligible population below 50 per cent of PL—less than 2 per cent in 2011-12.

Comparison among States

We also looked at the poverty ratios with different cut-offs of PLs for two relatively poorer states Bihar and Orissa and two developed states Tamil Nadu and Gujarat (Table 4.2). It provides interesting results. In the case of Bihar and Odisha, the rate of decline in poverty is lower for raised PLs of 125 per cent and 115 per cent as compared to PL and the lower cut-offs of 85 per cent and 75 per cent PL. The decline is even much faster for these two states at lower cut-offs if we take into account the base poverty ratio. The raised PLs for Orissa reveal only marginal decline for both 125 per cent and 115 per cent of PL. In the case of Gujarat, the decline in percentage points is higher for the raised cut-offs compared to lowered cut-offs. If we take into account the base effect, the rate of decline is higher for the lowered cut-offs. As far as Tamil Nadu is concerned, the decline in percentage points in poverty was higher for raised PL compared to those of lowered PLs. However, if we take the base effect, the rate of change is more or less similar.

Table 4.2

Poverty Ratios using Different Cut-offs: Total (Rural+Urban) for Four States

Poverty Line Cut-offs	*Bihar*		*Odisha*		*Gujarat*		*Tamil Nadu*	
	2009-10	*2011-12*	*2009-10*	*2011-12*	*2009-10*	*2011-12*	*2009-10*	*2011-12*
125% of PL	82.1	69.3	67.5	67.4	53.7	46.1	47.1	38.6
115% of PL	76.6	60.0	60.7	59.9	47.7	39.0	39.9	32.6
100% of PL	63.9	41.3	48.5	45.9	36.4	27.4	27.7	22.4
85% of PL	46.2	24.3	33.7	28.9	22.7	14.5	17.3	14.0
75% of PL	34.2	15.3	22.7	20.3	14.1	7.8	11.2	8.3
50% of PL	4.4	1.6	4.3	2.5	1.4	1.1	1.3	1.0

Source: Same as in Table 4.1.

As far as a concentration of poverty is concerned, it is clear that in all the four states bulk of the poor is between the PL and 75 per cent of the PL. In the case of two advanced states, Gujarat and Tamil Nadu, the concentration is even higher. In 2011-12, in Gujarat 71.5 per cent of the poor were within these limits. For the same year, in the case of Tamil Nadu, the percentage of the poor falling within these limits is 63 per cent. The proportions are however much lower in the case of Bihar and Odisha. In Bihar, it is 40.9 per cent and in Odisha it is 45.4 per cent. Unlike in the case of Bihar and Orissa, both in Gujarat and in Tamil Nadu the percentage of the poor falling between these limits has increased between 2009-10 and 2011-12 indicating a faster decline in the depth of poverty.

Where Do We Stand?

There are three conclusions from the all India and state-wise analysis. First, the rate of decline in poverty ratios for lowered cut-off is similar or more than those for PL or raised PL. Second, poverty is concentrated around the PL. Third, the percentage of population for 50 per cent of PL is negligible at all India and state level.

There is a considerable amount of debate on how to measure poverty. Prescribing a minimum level of income or consumption expenditure for defining poverty appears to be the most appropriate method. Obviously even with reference to the prescription of a minimum, there can be considerable differences of opinion. Our Committee in 2014 had set out a methodology for prescribing the minimum level of consumption expenditure of food and non-food items. The World Bank uses a single PL defined in terms of dollar and uses PPP exchange rate to derive each country's poverty line. This becomes inevitable when comparisons across countries have to be made. We must however recognise the limitations of such an exercise.

Bunching of poverty around the PL in our country renders the problem of reducing poverty more manageable. The pace and pattern of growth has a significant impact in reducing poverty ratios. But as we have repeatedly emphasised, policy makers must pursue a twofold strategy of letting the economy grow fast and attacking poverty directly through poverty alleviation programmes.

5

Report of the Expert Group to Review the Methodology for Measurement of Poverty

Table of Contents

Government of India, Planning Commission, June 2014.

Executive Summary

The apparent urgency with which the Expert Group (Rangarajan) has been formed reflects a need to examine the estimation of poverty in India keeping in mind the changed perceptions regarding the minimally acceptable standards of living in the country. Poverty lines estimated using the methodology provided by the Expert Group (Tendulkar) did not reflect the changing times and aspirations of the people of India. There was a need to re-examine the poverty line and its composition.

E.2 The methodology to measure poverty, as devised by Y.K. Alagh, in 1979 has been improvised by the Expert Group (Lakdawala) in 1993 and then by the Expert Group (Tendulkar) in 2009. The improvisations have led to a firmer reliance on the NSSO's sample surveys on consumption expenditure by households, a much better method to adjust for inter-state and inter-region differences in price changes over time, and the use of the better recall period introduced in the NSSO's surveys.

E.3 Issues in the measurement of poverty however, remain and this committee has taken a stand on these as follows:

i. The Expert Group (Tendulkar) had used the all-India urban poverty line basket as the reference to derive state-level rural and urban poverty. This was a departure from the earlier practice of using two separate poverty line baskets for rural and urban areas. The Expert Group (Rangarajan) reverts to the practice of having separate all-India rural and urban poverty basket lines and deriving state-level rural and urban estimates from these.

ii. The Expert Group (Tendulkar) had decided not to anchor the poverty line to the then available official calorie norms used in all poverty estimations since 1979 as it found a poor correlation between food consumed and nutrition outcomes. However, on a review of subsequent research, the Expert Group (Rangarajan) took a considered view that deriving the food component of the Poverty Line Basket by reference to the simultaneous satisfaction of all three nutrient-norms would be appropriate when seen in conjunction with the emphasis on a full range of policies and programmes for child-nutrition support and on public provisioning of a range of public goods and services aimed at the amelioration of the disease-environment facing the population.

iii. Estimates of consumption expenditure seen in the National Accounts Statistics and as inferred from the sample surveys of the National Sample Survey Organisation show a large and growing variance. The Expert Group (Rangarajan) prefers NSSO's estimates and decides not to use the NAS estimates. This is in line with the approach taken by Expert Group (Lakdawala) and Expert Group (Tendulkar).

iv. The capture of spatial and temporal variation in prices in estimating the State-level and rural-urban poverty levels (given all-India rural and urban estimates) has undergone substantial refinement since 1979. The Expert Group (Rangarajan) agrees with the methodology adopted by the Expert Group (Tendulkar) in this regard. This overcomes the limitations of using fixed base-year weights by using a combination of unit values derived from successive NSSO's Consumer Expenditure Surveys and price-relatives derived from the Consumer Price Indices.

v. Public expenditure on social services has increased substantially in recent years. These expenses are not captured, by design, in the NSSO's Consumer Expenditure Surveys and the poverty line derived from these is thus lower than the services actually consumed.

vi. The Expert Group (Rangarajan) is of the considered view that the deployment of criteria other than consumption expenditure in the measurement of poverty raises several issues regarding measurement and aggregation and that these render such exercises impractical. However, the Expert Group (Rangarajan) has considered an alternate view in estimating the poverty line by reference to the ability of households to save.

E.4 The methodology developed and adopted by the Expert Group (Rangarajan) and the results based on these are outlined below:

i. The poverty line should be based on certain normative levels of adequate nourishment, clothing, house rent, conveyance and education, and a behaviourally determined level of other non-food expenses.

ii. The Expert Group (Rangarajan) computed the average requirements of calories, proteins and fats based on ICMR norms differentiated by age, gender and activity for all-India rural and urban regions to derive the normative levels of nourishment. Accordingly, the energy requirement works out to 2,155 kcal per person per day in rural areas and 2,090 kcal per person per day in urban areas. For reasons elaborated in the text, the Expert Group (Rangarajan) views the Calorie norm not as a single number but as an average in a band of +/- 10 per cent of these values and with intakes even at the lower end still being adequate enough to not adversely affect health and work.

iii. The protein and fat requirements have been estimated on the same lines as for energy. These requirements are 48 gms and 28 gms per capita per day, respectively, in rural areas; and 50 gms and 26 gms per capita per day in urban areas.

iv. A food basket that simultaneously meets all the normative requirements of the three nutrients defines the food component of the poverty line basket proposed by the Expert Group (Rangarajan). These nutrient norms are met for persons located in the sixth fractile (25-30%) in rural areas and for those in the fourth fractile (15-20%) in urban areas in 2011-12. The average monthly per capita consumption expenditure on food in these fractile classes is ₹554 in rural areas and ₹656 in urban areas (NSS 68th Round).

v. The median fractile (45-50%) values of clothing expenses, rent, conveyance and education expenses are treated as the normative requirements of the basic non-food expenses of clothing, housing, mobility and education of a poverty line basket. This works out to ₹141 per capita per month in rural areas and ₹407 in urban areas. The observed expenses of all other non-food expenses of the fractile classes that meet the nutrition requirements are considered as part of the poverty line basket. This works out to ₹277 per capita per month in rural areas and ₹344 in urban areas.

vi. The new poverty line thus work out to monthly per capita consumption expenditure of ₹972 in rural areas and ₹1,407 in urban areas in 2011-12. For a family of five, this translates into a monthly consumption expenditure of ₹4,860 in rural areas and ₹7,035 in urban areas.

vii. Estimations of the poverty line made for the Expert Group (Rangarajan) based on an independent large survey of households by CMIE and using a different methodology wherein a household is considered poor if it is unable to save, yields results that are remarkably close to those derived using the NSSO data. This provides additional evidence in support of the poverty line derived by the Expert Group (Rangarajan).

viii. Compared to the poverty lines based on the methodology of the Expert Group (Tendulkar), the poverty lines estimated by the Expert Group (Rangarajan) are 19 per cent and 41 per cent higher in rural and urban areas, respectively. The Expert Group (Rangarajan) uses the Modified Mixed Recall Period consumption expenditure data of the NSSO as these are considered to be more precise compared to the MRP, which was used by the Expert Group (Tendulkar) and the URP, which was used by earlier estimations. 67 per cent of the increase in the rural poverty line and 28 per cent of the increase in the urban poverty line is because of the shift from MRP to MMRP.

ix. The national rural and urban poverty lines computed as above were used to derive the state-wise poverty lines by using the implicit price derived from the quantity and value of consumption observed in the NSSO's 68th Round of Consumer Expenditure Survey (2011-12) to estimate state relative to all-India Fisher price indices. Using these and the state-specific distribution of persons by expenditure groups (NSS), state-specific ratios of rural and urban poverty were estimated. State-level poverty ratio was estimated as weighted average of the rural and urban poverty ratios and the national poverty ratio was computed again as the population-weighted average of state-wise poverty ratios.

x. The Expert Group (Rangarajan) therefore estimates that the 30.9 per cent of the rural population and 26.4 per cent of the urban population was below the poverty line in 2011-12. The all-India ratio was 29.5 per cent. In rural India, 260.5 million individuals were below poverty and in urban India 102.5 million were under poverty. Totally, 363 million were below poverty in 2011-12.

xi. The poverty ratio has declined from 39.6 per cent in 2009-10 to 30.9 per cent in 2011-12 in rural India and from 35.1 per cent to 26.4 per cent in urban India. The decline was thus a uniform 8.7 percentage points over the two years. The all-India poverty ratio fell from 38.2 per cent to 29.5 per cent. Totally, 91.6 million individuals were lifted out of poverty during this period.

xii. The Expert Group (Rangarajan) recommends the updation of the poverty line in the future using the Fisher Index. The weighting diagram for this effort can be drawn from the NSSO's Consumer Expenditure Survey. For the Food–group, the Expert Group (Rangarajan) recommends that the current practice of relying on the unit values derivable from the NSSO Consumer Expenditure Surveys should continue till such time a new CPI of CSO with a weighting diagram based on the 2011-12 pattern of consumption becomes available. In respect of non-food items, the price indices available in the exiting CSO Consumer Price Indices can be used in the construction of requisite Fisher indices. Once the new series of Consumer Price Index numbers (with 2011-12 as the base year) become available, it may be used if the extent of change in the structure of consumption at that point in time relative to the 2011-12 structure of consumption is not very different.

1

The Background

The methodology for estimation of poverty used by the Planning Commission has been based on the recommendations made by Working Group/Task Force/Expert Groups consisting of eminent experts in the field. The Planning Commission has constituted these Groups from time to time to revisit the methodological issues related to the measurement of poverty so as to make the estimates more relevant to the contemporary economic situation. The methodology used by the Planning Commission at present (since January 2011) to estimate poverty is based on the recommendations of the Expert Group under the chairmanship of Prof Suresh D. Tendulkar.[1]

Within one and a half years of the acceptance of the recommendations of the Expert Group (Tendulkar), the Planning Commission in June 2012 constituted an Expert Group under the Chairmanship of Dr C. Rangarajan[2] to suggest a methodology for measurement of poverty with the following Terms of Reference:

(a) "To comprehensively review the existing methodology of estimation of poverty and examine whether the poverty line should be fixed solely in terms of a consumption basket or whether other criteria are also relevant, and if so, whether the two can be effectively combined to evolve a basis for estimation of poverty in rural and urban areas.

(b) To examine the issue of divergence between consumption estimates based on the NSSO methodology and those emerging from the National Accounts aggregates; and to suggest a methodology for updating consumption poverty lines using the new consumer price indices launched by the CSO for rural and urban areas state-wise.

(c) To review alternative methods of estimation of poverty which may be in use in other countries, including their procedural aspects; and indicate whether on this basis, a particular method can be evolved for empirical estimation of

1. Hereafter Expert Group (Tendulkar).
2. Hereafter Expert Group (Rangarajan).

poverty in India, including procedures for updating it over time and across states.

(d) To recommend how the estimates of poverty, as evolved above, should be linked to eligibility and entitlements for schemes and programmes under the Government of India".

In the past, the Planning Commission had constituted such Expert Groups after a gap of about 12 to 15 years. This is evident from the chronology of the constitution of the Expert Groups since 1962, the earliest attempt by the Planning Commission to devise a methodology of poverty estimation. The Working Group submitted its report in the same year and the Planning Commission accepted its recommendations immediately. Fifteen years after the Working Group, the Planning Commission constituted a Task Force in 1977 under the chairmanship of Dr Y.K. Alagh.[3] The Task Force submitted its report in 1979 and the Planning Commission accepted its recommendations in the same year. Twelve years after the constitution of the Task Force and ten years after the acceptance of its recommendations, the Planning Commission constituted an Expert Group in 1989 under the chairmanship of Prof D.T. Lakdawala.[4] The Expert Group (Lakdawala) submitted its report in 1993 and the Planning Commission accepted its recommendations in 1997. Then, 16 years after the constitution of the Expert Group (Lakdawala) and 8 years after the acceptance of its recommendations, the Planning Commission constituted the Expert Group under the chairmanship of Prof Suresh D. Tendulkar in 2005. The Expert Group (Tendulkar) submitted its report in November 2009 and the Planning Commission accepted its recommendations in January 2011. The Expert Group (Rangarajan) has been constituted seven years after the constitution of the Expert Group (Tendulkar), less than three years after the submission of its recommendations and only one and a half years after the acceptance of its recommendations. It is therefore apparent that the Planning Commission has demonstrated a greater urgency than in the past in constituting a new Expert Group (Rangarajan).

3. Hereafter Task Force (Alagh).

4. Hereafter Expert Group (Lakdawala).

The methodology of the Expert Group (Tendulkar) generically belongs to its predecessors, namely the Working Group of 1962, the Task Force of 1979 and the Expert Group in 1993. Its methodology is based on an exogenously determined poverty line expressed in terms of per capita consumption expenditure in a month and the class distribution of NSS (National Sample Survey) consumer expenditure data of the National Sample Survey Office (NSSO). The poverty ratio (percentage of people living below the poverty line) is obtained by counting the persons lying below the poverty line from the class distribution of persons.

There is an estimate of the poverty line, quantified by the Task Force in 1979. The Task Force poverty lines (estimated at the national level, separately in rural and urban areas) were adopted by the Expert Group (Lakdawala) and used in the estimation of poverty after disaggregating the national poverty line into state-specific poverty lines. The Expert Group (Tendulkar) adopted the national urban poverty line (the latest available for the year 2004-05) derived by the Planning Commission using the Expert Group (Lakdawala) methodology and equated this for the entire country. Then, it employed a different method of pricing the goods and services constituting the consumption basket of the poor (from the one used by the Expert Group, Lakdawala, and then used by the Planning Commission), and in essence, the poverty line. The Expert Group (Tendulkar) validated the poverty lines by checking the adequacy of actual private consumption expenditure per capita near the poverty line on food, education and health by comparing them with normative expenditures consistent with nutritional, educational and health outcomes respectively.

The poverty lines defined by the Tendulkar Committee did not reflect the changing times and aspirations of the people. The high rate of increase in per capita income and consumption in the first decade of this century and the consequential changes in the structure of the economy as well as in people's perspectives on poverty was viewed as requiring a fresh look at the poverty line and its composition. This provides the backdrop to the setting up of the Expert Group (Rangarajan).

2

Evolution of Measurement of Poverty in India

The Planning Commission is the nodal agency in the Government of India for estimation of poverty. It estimates the incidence of poverty at the national and state level separately in rural and urban areas. The incidence of poverty is measured by the poverty ratio, which is the ratio of number of poor to the total population expressed as percentage. It is also known as head-count ratio. The poverty ratio is measured from an exogenously determined poverty line quantified in terms of per capita consumption expenditure over a month and the class distribution of persons obtained from the large sample survey of consumer expenditure data of the NSSO.

After the Working Group of the Planning Commission delineated the methodology of poverty estimation in 1962, it has been intensely debated by the academicians, experts, policy planners, etc. over the years. In response, the Planning Commission has constituted Task Force/Expert Group from time to time to review the methodology. These include the Task Force under the chairmanship of Dr Y.K. Alagh in 1977; the Expert Groups under the chairmanship of Prof D.T. Lakdawala in 1989 and Prof S.D. Tendulkar in 2005. This chapter takes a look at the evolution of the methodology of measurement of poverty as recommended by the Working Group 1962, Task Force (Alagh), Expert Group (Lakdawala) and Expert Group (Tendulkar).

Working Group (1962)

The Planning Commission constituted a Working Group in 1962 to find out a desirable minimum level of living for the population. The Working Group recommended that the national minimum consumption expenditure for a household of five persons (four adult consumption units) should be not less than ₹100 per month or ₹20 per capita per month in terms of 1960-61 prices. For urban areas, this figure was ₹125 per month or ₹25 per capita per month to cover the higher prices there. The poverty line excluded expenditure on health and education, both of which, it was assumed, were to be provided by the State.

The Working Group (1962) appeared to have taken into account the recommendation of balanced diet made by the Nutrition Advisory Group of the Indian Council of Medical Research (ICMR) in 1958. This poverty line was widely used in the 1960s and 1970s to estimate the poverty ratio at national and state level.

Task Force 1979: Alagh

The Planning Commission in July 1977 constituted the Task Force on "Projections of Minimum Needs and Effective Consumption Demand" under the Chairmanship of Dr Y.K. Alagh. The Task Force submitted its report in January 1979 and the Planning Commission accepted its recommendations in the same month. The Task Force provided a quantitative measure of poverty by estimating:

(a) The average calorie requirements were estimated, separately for the all-India rural and urban areas as a population-weighted average of the age-gender-activity specific calorie allowances recommended by the Nutrition Expert Group (1968) by reference to the 1971 population Census.

(b) The poverty line corresponding to the calorie requirement

The estimated calorie norm was 2400 kcal per capita per day in rural areas and 2100 kcal per capita per day in urban areas. To work out the monetary equivalent of these norms, 28th Round (1973-74) NSS data relating to household consumption both in quantitative and value terms were used. Based on the observed consumer behaviour in 1973-74 it was estimated that, on an average, consumer expenditure (food and non-food) of ₹49.09 per capita per month was associated with a calorie intake of 2400 per capita per day in rural areas and ₹56.64 per capita per month with a calorie intake of 2100 per day in urban areas. This Monthly Per Capita Expenditure (MPCE) was termed as poverty line. The poverty lines for later years were estimated by updating the poverty lines of the year 1973-74 for price changes.

The Task Force used the percentage distribution of persons in different expenditure classes in the NSS data on household consumer expenditure to estimate the percentage of persons living below the poverty line. The NSS distribution of private consumption was adjusted pro-rata to correspond to the consumption estimates of National Accounts Statistics (NAS) made by the Central Statistical Office (CSO). Using the poverty line and the adjusted distribution of persons by expenditure classes for the reference year the percentage of persons below the poverty line was estimated. Applying the projected population of the year, the number of persons in poverty was estimated from the percentage of persons. The poverty line was defined at national level (separately for rural and urban areas).

The poverty line defined by the Task Force at 1973-74 prices was updated by the Planning Commission (to estimate poverty for a later year) using the implicit CSO private consumption expenditure deflator. CSO in their national accounts publish the estimates of expenditure at current and constant prices. The ratio between the two yields the consumption deflator. Planning Commission used national poverty line uniformly for all states and Union Territories (UTs) to estimate.

Estimation of poverty by the Planning Commission following Task Force methodology, as is seen above, is based on the national poverty line and pro-rata adjustment of the NSS consumption expenditure to NAS consumption across all expenditure groups of the population. The adjustment whereby the discrepancy between the NAS and the NSS estimates of consumption is allocated on a pro-rata basis across all expenditure classes was debated by experts mainly because the discrepancy grew in later years and also because the discrepancy could not possibly be similar across all consumption expenditure deciles of the population. Besides, it was pointed out that the application of a single poverty line for all the states (though separate in rural and urban areas) implicitly, and dubiously assumes absence of price differential across the states. The estimate of poverty based on this methodology also assumed a fixed consumption basket of the poor overtime, and a uniform consumption basket for all the states.

The Planning Commission methodology for estimating poverty at national and state level was regarded by some as inappropriate in giving a representative picture of the incidence of poverty in the country. The main points of the criticism were:

(a) the adjustment procedure;
(b) the choice of deflators to represent price changes in the poverty line;
(c) application of the same poverty line in all the states, which imply the absence of price differentials across the states;
(d) use of a fixed consumption basket over time; and
(e) the uniform consumption basket for all the states.

The magnitude of poverty ratio based on this methodology fell significantly as the adjustment factor (i.e. the difference between the NSS and the NAS consumption) increased overtime. A lower level of poverty leads to a lower allocation not only in the anti-poverty programmes, but also in the developmental programmes, as the latter also takes poverty as one of the criteria in its allocation, both inter- and intra-state. Faced with these odds, the Planning Commission constituted the Expert Group under the Chairmanship of Prof D.T. Lakdawala to re-visit the methodology of poverty estimation.

Expert Group 1993: Lakdawala

The Planning Commission, in September 1989, constituted the Expert Group on Estimation of Proportion and Number of Poor to "look into the methodology for estimation of poverty and to re-define the poverty line, if necessary". The Expert Group submitted its Report in July 1993. The Government accepted the Expert Group methodology in March 1997 as the basis for computing the official estimates of poverty in India.

The Expert Group (Lakdawala) did not redefine the poverty line. It retained the one defined by the Task Force (Alagh) which was at national level in rural and urban areas. It disaggregated these national poverty lines into state-specific poverty lines in order to reflect the inter-state price differentials.

i. The national rural poverty line of Task Force (Alagh) was disaggregated into state-specific poverty lines using inter-state price differentials measured by Fisher's Index. These state-specific poverty lines of base year (1973-74) were updated for subsequent years using state-specific price indices especially constructed by taking weighted average of the commodity group-wise Consumer Price Index of Agricultural Labourers (CPIAL) of (a) food, (b) fuel and light, (c) clothing and footwear, and (d) miscellaneous with their respective weights in the national consumption basket of the poor in 1973-74.

ii. The national urban poverty line of the Task Force was disaggregated into state-specific poverty lines in a similar way as in the case of the rural poverty line using state-specific price indices and inter-state price differentials. The state-specific price indices were constructed by taking weighted average of the commodity group-wise Consumer Price Index of Industrial Workers (CPIIW) of (a) food, (b) fuel and light, (c) housing, (d) clothing, bedding and footwear, and (e) miscellaneous with their respective weights in the national consumption basket of the poor in 1973-74.

iii. The national (All-India) poverty line in the Expert Group (Lakdawala) method was worked out as an interpolated value from the national consumption distribution obtained from the NSS consumer expenditure data and the national poverty ratio. The national poverty ratio was estimated as a population-weighted average of the state-wise poverty ratios, separately for rural and urban areas.

The Expert Group (Lakdawala) calculated the state specific poverty ratios in rural and urban areas from the state-specific poverty lines and the state-specific distribution of persons by expenditure groups obtained from large sample surveys on household consumer expenditure of the NSSO, which are available once in approximately five years. The NSS consumption distribution was used as it is, that is without adjustment to the NAS consumption. This was a major departure from the Task Force method, which did this adjustment on a pro-rata basis. The aggregate poverty ratio of the state was worked out by combining its rural and urban poverty ratios. The national poverty ratio was computed as weighted average of state-wise poverty ratios.

The Expert Group (Lakdawala) could estimate the poverty lines in rural and urban areas of eighteen States. These eighteen states are: Andhra Pradesh, Assam, Bihar, Gujarat, Haryana, Himachal Pradesh, Jammu and Kashmir, Karnataka, Kerala, Madhya Pradesh, Maharashtra, Orissa, Punjab, Rajasthan, Tamil Nadu, Uttar Pradesh, West Bengal and Delhi. In the remaining States/UTs, the poverty lines could not be computed similarly because of non-availability of state-specific prices data. In these States, the poverty ratios were equated with one of these eighteen states based on the criteria of physical contiguity of areas and similarity of economic profile. This resulted in the adoption of (a) the poverty ratio of Assam for Arunachal Pradesh, Meghalaya, Mizoram, Manipur, Nagaland, Tripura and Sikkim; (b) the poverty ratio of Tamil Nadu for Pondicherry and Andaman and Nicobar Islands; (c) the poverty ratio of Kerala for Lakshadweep; (d) the poverty ratio of Goa for Daman and Diu; (e) Urban poverty ratio of Punjab for both rural and urban areas of Chandigarh.

Two factors largely distinguish the Expert Group (Lakdawala) methodology of poverty estimation from those of the Task Force (Alagh). First, the Expert Group (Lakdawala) method uses state-specific poverty lines as against national poverty line for estimation of poverty in the state; it thereby captures the cost of living in the states more accurately (as compared to the Task Force method). Second, the Expert Group (Lakdawala) uses the state-wise consumption distribution of the NSS without any adjustment to the NAS consumption. This is a major departure from the Task Force method, which did this adjustment on a pro-rata basis.

In March 1997, the Government adopted the Expert Group (Lakdawala) methodology for poverty estimation as the basis for computing the official estimates of poverty and using this methodology the Planning Commission estimated the poverty ratios in rural and urban areas of different States/UTs for the year 1973-74 (NSS 28th Round consumer expenditure data, which was used to estimate the poverty line by the Task Force), and for the years 1977-1978, 1983, 1987-88 and 1993-94 for which the large sample survey consumer expenditure data were then available from the 32nd, 38th, 43rd and 50th Rounds of the NSS.[5] Subsequently, using the same

5. Government of India, Press Information Bureau, 11th March 1997.

methodology the Planning Commission estimated the poverty ratios at the national and states level for the years 1999-2000 and 2004-05, using the NSS large sample survey consumer expenditure data of 55th and 61st Rounds respectively.[6]

The official estimate of poverty was derived by the Planning Commission using the Expert Group (Lakdawala) methodology until January 2011. The poverty ratio (i.e., the percentage of people living below the poverty line) and the number of poor for different years at the national level estimated from the Expert Group (Lakdawala) method are given in Table 1.

Table 1

Poverty Ratio and Number of Poor: Expert Group (Lakdawala) Method

Year	*Poverty Ratio (%)*			*Number of Poor (million)*		
	Rural	*Urban*	*Total*	*Rural*	*Urban*	*Total*
1973-74	56.4	49.0	54.9	261.3	60.0	321.3
1977-78	53.1	45.2	51.3	264.3	64.6	328.9
1983	45.7	40.8	44.5	252.0	70.9	322.9
1987-88	39.1	38.2	38.9	231.9	75.2	307.1
1993-94	37.3	32.4	36.0	244.0	76.3	320.3
2004-05 (URP)	28.3	25.7	27.5	220.9	80.8	301.7

Note: N.B.: URP = URP consumption = Uniform Recall Period consumption in which the consumer expenditure data for all the items are collected from 30 day recall period.

The state-specific poverty line and poverty ratio estimated from the Expert Group (Lakdawala) method and used as the official measure of poverty until January 2011 are given in Annexure-A.

Expert Group (Tendulkar)

The Expert Group under the chairmanship of Suresh D. Tendulkar was constituted by the Planning Commission in December 2005. It was mandated to: (a) examine the issues relating to the comparability of the NSS 50th (1993-94), NSS 55th (1999-2000) and NSS 61st (2004-05) Round consumer expenditure data and suggest methodologies for deriving such comparability with past and future

6. Government of India, Press Information Bureau, 22nd February 2001 and Government of India, Press Information Bureau, 21st March 2007.

survey data; (b) review alternative conceptualisations of poverty, and associated technical aspects of procedures of measurement and data base for empirical estimation including procedures for updating over time and across states, and (c) recommend any changes in the existing procedures of official estimates of poverty. The Expert Group (Tendulkar) submitted its recommendations to the Planning Commission in November 2009.[7]

The Expert Group (Tendulkar) did not construct a poverty line. It adopted the officially measured urban poverty line of 2004-05 based on Expert Group (Lakdawala) methodology and converted this poverty line (which is URP-consumption based) into MRP-consumption.[8] The method of estimation of poverty line and poverty ratio suggested by the Expert Group (Tendulkar) is described in the following three steps.

Step 1: Convert the URP-consumption based urban poverty line into MRP-consumption based poverty line (MRP distribution = consumer expenditure data is collected using 365-day recall period for five non-food items *viz.*, clothing, footwear, durable goods, education and institutional medical expenses, and 30-day recall period for the remaining items). Here, the MRP-consumption based urban poverty line is worked out as the level of per capita consumption expenditure in the MRP consumption distribution that corresponds to the bottom 25.7 per cent of the population, which is the official urban poverty ratio derived from the Expert Group (Lakdawala) methodology using the poverty line and the class distribution of consumption, both based on URP-consumption.

7. Report of the Expert Group to Review the Methodology for Estimation of Poverty, Planning Commission, November, 2009, downloaded from : *http://planningcommission.gov.in*

8. URP-consumption = consumption data are collected from the households using 30 day recall period for all the items. MRP-consumption = consumption data for five non-food items *viz.*, clothing, footwear, durable goods, education, and institutional medical expenses are collected using 365-day recall period and 30-day recall period for the remaining items.

Step 2: State-specific urban poverty lines are derived from the (MRP-consumption based) national urban poverty line using urban state-relative-to-all-India fisher indices.[9]

Step 3: The state-specific rural poverty lines are worked out from the state-specific urban poverty lines by applying within-state rural-relative-to-urban Fisher indices.[10]

Here, the state index numbers relative to the all-India numbers and the state-specific rural prices relative to the state-specific urban prices are computed from the implicit price indices derived from the quantity and value of different items of consumer expenditure gathered in the NSS consumption expenditure.

The state-specific poverty ratios are estimated from the state-specific class distribution of persons obtained from the MRP-consumption distribution of the NSS consumer expenditure and the state-specific poverty line. The national poverty ratio is estimated as a weighted average of state-wise poverty ratios.

The national urban poverty ratio in 2004-05 as per the Expert Group (Tendulkar) methodology is identical to the one estimated by the Expert Group (Lakdawala) methodology, which is 25.7 per cent. The shift from MPCE estimates on URP (that underlay the poverty ratio with the Lakdawala methodology) to those on MRP in the Expert Group (Tendulkar) methodology significantly raised the all-India Urban poverty line level of MPCE from 538.60 to ₹578.80. Associated with this higher cut-off level of MPCE is also

9. This national level urban poverty line is disaggregated into state-specific poverty lines using "urban state-relative-to-all-India" price differentials. The prices differentials are constructed from a variety of price data most of which are implicit. For 15 commodity groups namely cereals, pulses, milk, oil, egg-fish-meat, vegetables, fresh-fruit, dry-fruit, sugar, salt-spices, other-food, intoxicants, fuel-light, clothing & bedding and footwear, the Fisher indices are computed using implicit prices obtained from the NSS consumer expenditure data of 61st Round (2004-05); for five item groups namely entertainment, personal care items, miscellaneous goods, miscellaneous services and durables, Labour Bureau price data underlying CPIAL and CPIIW is used. The pricing of educational services are constructed from the employment-unemployment survey of the NSS 61st Round (2004-05) and of health services are constructed from the health and morbidity survey of NSS 60th Round (January–June 2004).

10. The state-specific rural poverty lines (of 2004-05) are worked out by adjusting the state-specific urban poverty lines (of 2004-05) with the "within-state rural-relative-to-urban" price differentials computed from the similar price statistics as in the case of disaggregating the national poverty line into state-specific poverty lines in urban areas.

different poverty line basket (PLB) as compared to that underlying the all-India urban poverty ratio as per Expert Group (Lakdawala). All other poverty lines for the rural and urban areas of individual states proposed by the Expert Group (Tendulkar) are aligned to this new PLB at a higher level of MPCE. In Tendulkar Committee report, it is stated that:

> As urban living standard is generally regarded as better than and preferable to its rural counterpart, this Expert Group recommends that the purchasing power represented by the MRP equivalent PCTE underlying the all-India HCR of 25.7 per cent be taken as the new reference PLB for measuring poverty and made available to both the rural and urban population in all the states after correcting for urban-rural price differentials as well as urban and rural state-relative-to all-India price differentials.

In the Expert Group (Tendulkar) methodology, the all-India rural poverty ratio is obtained in the same way as in the Expert Group (Lakdawala). The all-India rural poverty ratio so derived, at 41.8 per cent is one and a half times the estimate of Expert Group (Lakdawala) which was 28.3 per cent.

A key element in the Expert Group(Tendulkar) methodology is the derivation of the reference All-India poverty line basket(PLB) as one corresponding to the MRP- equivalent of MPCE corresponding to the all-India urban HCR on URP as per the Expert Group (Lakdawala) methodology. It asserts that "the urban proportion (of 25.7 per cent) is less controversial in terms of the broad order of magnitude of extent of poverty". The phrase "less controversial" is to be seen in the context of its observation that "the latest official estimate of rural poverty is widely perceived to be too low". While two reasons are advanced in respect of its observation on rural HCR: (i) understated price-adjustment and (ii) "its basis of a very old and out-dated 1973-74 poverty line basket", the assertion about the corresponding urban HCR as being "less controversial" remains just that: an assertion without any evidence or reasoning. Other analysts have estimated urban poverty levels different from the official estimates.

The Expert Group (Tendulkar) outlined the methodology for updation of the state-specific rural and urban poverty lines of

2004-05 for future years. (The updation is carried out by adjusting the urban state-specific poverty lines of 2004-05 with the Fisher index of changes in state-level urban prices between 2004-05 and later years (for example, 2009-10 and 2011-12) to derive state-level urban poverty lines for later years. Thereafter, the state specific rural poverty lines for later years are derived by applying the within-state rural-relative-to-urban Fisher indices to updated urban poverty lines.

The Planning Commission released estimates of poverty for 1993-94 and 2004-05 derived from the Expert Group (Tendulkar) method In January 2011. Subsequently, based on the same methodology, the poverty ratio for 2009-10 and 2011-12 were derived by the Planning Commission in March 2012 and July 2013 respectively. The estimate of poverty ratio and number of poor at the national level for the years 1993-94, 2004-05, 2009-10 and 2011-12 derived from the Expert Group (Tendulkar) methodology are given in Table 2. The rate of decline in poverty ratio during different period is given in Table 3.

Table 2

Percentage and Number of Poor Estimated from Expert Group (Tendulkar) Methodology

	Year	*Poverty Ratio (%)*			*Number of Poor (million)*		
		Rural	*Urban*	*Total*	*Rural*	*Urban*	*Total*
1.	1993-94	50.1	31.8	45.3	328.6	74.5	403.7
2.	2004-05	41.8	25.7	37.2	326.3	80.8	407.1
3.	2009-10	33.8	20.9	29.8	278.2	76.5	354.7
4.	2011-12	25.7	13.7	21.9	216.7	53.1	269.8

Table 3

Decline in Poverty Ratio Estimated from Expert Group (Tendulkar) Methodology

(Percentage points per year)

	Period	*Rural*	*Urban*	*Total*
a)	1993-94 to 2004-05	0.75	0.55	0.74
b)	2004-05 to 2011-12	2.32	1.69	2.18
c)	1993-94 to 2011-12	1.36	1.01	1.30

The state-wise estimate of the poverty line and poverty ratio for the years 1993-94, 2004-05, 2009-10 and 2011-12 derived from the Expert Group (Tendulkar) methodology are given in Annexure-B.

Annexure-A

Table A-1

State Specific Poverty Lines in Rural Areas (Lakdawala Methodology)

(₹ monthly per capita)

S. No.	*States/UTs*	*1973-74*	*1977-78*	*1983-84*	*1987-88*	*1993-94*	*1999-2000*	*2004-05*
1.	Andhra Pradesh	41.71	50.88	72.66	91.94	163.02	262.94	292.95
2.	Arunachal Pradesh	*	*	*	*	*	*	*
3.	Assam	49.82	60.29	98.32	127.44	232.05	365.43	387.64
4.	Bihar	57.68	58.93	97.48	120.36	212.16	333.07	354.36
5.	Chhattisgarh							322.41
6.	Goa	50.47	58.07	88.24	115.61	194.94	318.63	362.25
7.	Gujarat	47.10	54.70	83.29	115.00	202.11	318.94	353.93
8.	Haryana	49.95	59.37	88.57	122.90	233.79	362.81	414.76
9.	Himachal Pradesh	49.95	59.37	88.57	122.90	233.79	367.45	394.28
10.	Jammu & Kashmir	46.59	61.53	91.75	124.33	*	367.45	391.26
11.	Jharkhand							366.56
12.	Karnataka	47.24	51.95	83.31	104.46	186.63	309.59	324.17
13.	Kerala	51.68	58.88	99.35	130.61	243.84	374.79	430.12
14.	Madhya Pradesh	50.20	56.26	83.59	107.00	193.10	311.34	327.78
15.	Maharashtra	50.47	58.07	88.24	115.61	194.94	318.63	362.25
16.	Manipur	*	*	*	*	*	*	*
17.	Meghalaya	*	*	*	*	*	*	*
18.	Mizoram	*	*	*	*	*	*	*
19.	Nagaland	*	*	*	*	*	*	*
20.	Orissa	46.87	58.89	106.28	121.42	194.03	323.92	325.79
21.	Punjab	49.95	59.37	88.57	122.90	233.79	362.68	410.38
22.	Rajasthan	50.96	57.54	80.24	117.52	215.89	344.03	374.57
23.	Sikkim	*	*	*	*	*	*	*
24.	Tamil Nadu	45.09	56.62	96.15	118.23	196.53	307.64	351.86
25.	Tripura	*	*	*	*	*	*	*
26.	Uttar Pradesh	48.92	54.21	83.85	114.57	213.01	336.88	365.84
27.	Uttarakhand							478.02

28.	West Bengal	54.49	63.34	105.55	129.21	220.74	350.17	382.82
29.	A & N Island	*	*	*	*	*	*	*
30.	Chandigarh	*	*	*	*	*	*	*
31.	Dadra & Nagar Haveli	50.47	58.07	88.24	115.61	194.94	318.63	362.25
32.	Daman & Diu	*	*	*	*	*	*	*
33.	Delhi	49.95	59.37	88.57	122.90	233.79	362.68	410.38
34.	Lakshadweep	*	*	*	*	*	*	*
35.	Pondicherry	*	*	*	*	*	*	*
	All India#	49.63	56.84	89.50	115.20	205.84	327.56	356.3

Notes: * In the Expert Group, poverty ratios for these states have not been calculated separately, but have been adopted from those of other states.

The poverty line (implicit) at all-India level is worked out from the expenditure class-wise distribution of persons and the poverty ratio at all-India level. The poverty ratio at all-India level is obtained as weighted average of the state-wise poverty ratio.

Table A-2

State Specific Poverty Lines in Urban Areas (Lakdawala Methodology)

(₹ monthly per capita)

S. No.	*States/UTs*	*1973-74*	*1977-78*	*1983-84*	*1987-88*	*1993-94*	*1999-2000*	*2004-05*
1.	Andhra Pradesh	53.96	69.05	106.43	151.88	278.14	457.40	542.89
2.	Arunachal Pradesh	*	*	*	*	*	*	*
3.	Assam	50.26	61.38	97.51	126.60	212.42	343.99	378.84
4.	Bihar	61.27	67.27	111.80	150.25	238.49	379.78	435.00
5.	Chhattisgarh							560.00
6.	Goa	59.48	73.99	126.47	189.17	328.56	539.71	665.90
7.	Gujarat	62.17	72.39	123.22	173.18	297.22	474.41	541.16
8.	Haryana	52.42	66.94	103.48	143.22	258.23	420.20	504.49
9.	Himachal Pradesh	51.93	66.32	102.26	144.10	253.61	420.20	504.49
10.	Jammu & Kashmir	37.17	55.41	99.62	148.38	*	420.20	553.77
11.	Jharkhand							451.24
12.	Karnataka	58.22	68.85	120.19	171.18	302.89	511.44	599.66
13.	Kerala	62.78	67.05	122.64	163.29	280.54	477.06	559.39
14.	Madhya Pradesh	63.02	74.40	122.82	178.35	317.16	481.65	570.15
15.	Maharashtra	59.48	73.99	126.47	189.17	328.56	539.71	665.90
16.	Manipur	*	*	*	*	*	*	*

contd...

...contd

17.	Meghalaya	*	*	*	*	*	*	*
18.	Mizoram	*	*	*	*	*	*	*
19.	Nagaland	*	*	*	*	*	*	*
20.	Orissa	59.34	72.41	124.81	165.40	298.22	473.12	528.49
21.	Punjab	51.93	65.70	101.03	144.98	253.61	388.15	466.16
22.	Rajasthan	59.99	72.00	113.55	165.38	280.85	465.92	559.63
23.	Sikkim	*	*	*	*	*	*	*
24.	Tamil Nadu	51.54	67.02	120.30	165.82	296.63	475.60	547.42
25.	Tripura	*	*	*	*	*	*	*
26.	Uttar Pradesh	57.37	69.66	110.23	154.15	258.65	416.29	483.26
27.	Uttarakhand							637.67
28.	West Bengal	54.81	67.50	105.91	149.96	247.53	409.22	449.32
29.	A & N Island	*	*	*	*	*	*	*
30.	Chandigarh	*	*	*	*	*	*	*
31.	Dadra & Nagar Haveli	59.48	73.99	126.47	189.17	328.56	539.71	665.90
32.	Daman & Diu	*	*	*	*	*	*	*
33.	Delhi	67.95	80.17	123.29	176.91	309.48	505.45	612.91
34.	Lakshadweep	*	*	*	*	*	*	*
35.	Pondicherry	*	*	*	*	*	*	*
	All India#	56.76	70.33	115.65	162.16	281.35	454.11	538.60

Notes: * In the Expert Group, poverty ratios for these states have not been calculated separately, but have been adopted from those of other states.

The poverty line(implicit) at all-India level is worked out from the expenditure class-wise distribution of persons and the poverty ratio at all-India level. The poverty ratio at all-India level is obtained as weighted average of the state-wise poverty ratio.

Table A-3

Number and Percentage of Population Below Poverty Line by States, 1973-74 (Lakdawala Methodology)

S. No.	*States/UTs*	*Rural*		*Urban*		*Total*	
		No. of Persons (Lakhs)	*% of Persons*	*No. of Persons (Lakhs)*	*% of Persons*	*No. of Persons (Lakhs)*	*% of Persons*
1.	Andhra Pradesh	178.21	48.41	47.48	50.61	225.69	48.86
2.	Arunachal Pradesh	2.57	52.67	0.09	36.92	2.66	51.93
3.	Assam	76.37	52.67	5.46	36.92	81.83	51.21
4.	Bihar	336.52	62.99	34.05	52.96	370.57	61.91

5.	Goa	3.16	46.85	1.00	37.69	4.16	44.26
6.	Gujarat	94.61	46.35	43.81	52.57	138.42	48.15
7.	Haryana	30.08	34.23	8.24	40.18	38.32	35.36
8.	Himachal Pradesh	9.38	27.42	0.35	13.17	9.73	26.39
9.	Jammu & Kashmir	18.41	45.51	2.07	21.32	20.48	40.83
10.	Karnataka	128.4	55.14	42.27	52.53	170.67	54.47
11.	Kerala	111.36	59.19	24.16	62.74	135.52	59.79
12.	Madhya Pradesh	231.21	62.66	45.09	57.65	276.30	61.78
13.	Maharashtra	210.84	57.71	76.58	43.87	287.42	53.24
14.	Manipur	5.11	52.67	0.75	36.92	5.86	49.96
15.	Meghalaya	4.88	52.67	0.64	36.92	5.52	50.20
16.	Mizoram	1.62	52.67	0.20	36.92	1.82	50.32
17.	Nagaland	2.65	52.67	0.25	36.92	2.90	50.81
18.	Orissa	142.24	67.28	12.23	55.62	154.47	66.18
19.	Punjab	30.47	28.21	10.02	27.96	40.49	28.15
20.	Rajasthan	101.41	44.76	27.10	52.13	128.51	46.14
21.	Sikkim	1.09	52.67	0.10	36.92	1.19	50.86
22.	Tamil Nadu	172.6	57.43	66.92	49.40	239.52	54.94
23.	Tripura	7.88	52.67	0.66	36.92	8.54	51.00
24.	Uttar Pradesh	449.99	56.53	85.74	60.09	535.73	57.07
25.	West Bengal	257.96	73.16	41.34	34.67	299.30	63.43
26.	A & N Island	0.59	57.43	0.15	49.40	0.74	55.56
27.	Chandigarh	0.07	27.96	0.77	27.96	0.84	27.96
28.	Dadra & Nagar Haveli	0.37	46.85	0.01	37.69	0.38	46.55
29.	Delhi	1.06	24.44	21.78	52.23	22.84	49.61
30.	Lakshadweep	0.18	59.19	0.03	62.74	0.21	59.68
31.	Pondicherry	1.61	57.43	1.13	49.40	2.74	53.82
	All India	2612.90	56.44	600.46	49.01	3213.36	54.88

Notes: 1. Poverty Ratio of Assam is used for Sikkim, Arunachal Pradesh, Meghalaya, Mizoram, Manipur, Nagaland and Tripura.

2. Poverty Ratio of Tamil Nadu is used for Pondicherry and Andaman & Nicobar Island.
3. Poverty Ratio of Kerala is used for Lakshadweep.
4. Poverty Ratio of Goa is used for Dadra & Nagar Haveli.
5. Urban Poverty Ratio of Punjab used for both rural and urban poverty of Chandigarh.
6. Poverty Line of Maharashtra and expenditure distribution of Goa is used to estimate poverty ratio of Goa.

Table A-4

Number and Percentage of Population Below Poverty Line by States, 1977-78 (Lakdawala Methodology)

S. No.	States/UTs	Rural		Urban		Total	
		No. of Persons (Lakhs)	% of Persons	No. of Persons (Lakhs)	% of Persons	No. of Persons (Lakhs)	% of Persons
1.	Andhra Pradesh	149.13	38.11	48.41	43.55	197.54	39.31
2.	Arunachal Pradesh	3.26	59.82	0.10	32.71	3.36	58.32
3.	Assam	97.55	59.82	5.83	32.71	103.38	57.15
4.	Bihar	364.48	63.25	37.34	48.76	401.82	61.55
5.	Goa	2.72	37.64	1.16	36.31	3.88	37.23
6.	Gujarat	92.53	41.76	38.35	40.02	130.88	41.23
7.	Haryana	26.43	27.73	9.05	36.57	35.48	29.55
8.	Himachal Pradesh	12.46	33.49	0.58	19.44	13.04	32.45
9.	Jammu & Kashmir	19.04	42.86	2.68	23.71	21.72	38.97
10.	Karnataka	120.39	48.18	47.78	50.36	168.17	48.78
11.	Kerala	102.85	51.48	24.37	55.62	127.22	52.22
12.	Madhya Pradesh	247.98	62.52	54.89	58.66	302.87	61.78
13.	Maharashtra	249.75	63.97	80.16	40.09	329.91	55.88
14.	Manipur	6.09	59.82	0.97	32.71	7.06	53.72
15.	Meghalaya	6.10	59.82	0.69	32.71	6.79	55.19
16.	Mizoram	2.03	59.82	0.28	32.71	2.31	54.38
17.	Nagaland	3.44	59.82	0.30	32.71	3.74	56.04
18.	Orissa	162.50	72.38	13.82	50.92	176.32	70.07
19.	Punjab	18.87	16.37	11.36	27.32	30.23	19.27
20.	Rajasthan	89.66	35.89	27.22	43.53	116.88	37.42
21.	Sikkim	1.41	59.82	0.13	32.71	1.54	55.89
22.	Tamil Nadu	182.50	57.68	72.97	48.69	255.47	54.79
23.	Tripura	9.95	59.82	0.66	32.71	10.61	56.88
24.	Uttar Pradesh	407.41	47.60	96.96	56.23	504.37	49.05
25.	West Bengal	259.69	68.34	50.88	38.20	310.57	60.52
26.	A & N Island	0.71	57.68	0.20	48.69	0.91	55.42
27.	Chandigarh	0.08	27.32	0.95	27.32	1.03	27.32

28.	Dadra & Nagar Haveli	0.33	37.64	0.16	36.31	0.49	37.20
29.	Delhi	1.35	30.19	16.81	33.51	18.16	33.23
30.	Lakshadweep	0.13	51.48	0.07	55.62	0.20	52.79
31.	Pondicherry	1.65	57.68	1.35	48.69	3.00	53.25
	All India	2642.47	53.07	646.48	45.24	3288.95	51.32

Notes: 1. Poverty Ratio of Assam is used for Sikkim, Arunachal Pradesh, Meghalaya, Mizoram, Manipur, Nagaland and Tripura.

2. Poverty Ratio of Tamil Nadu is used for Pondicherry and A & N Island.
3. Poverty Ratio of Kerala is used for Lakshadweep.
4. Poverty Ratio of Goa is used for Dadra & Nagar Haveli.
5. Urban Poverty Ratio of Punjab is used for both rural and urban poverty of Chandigarh.
6. Poverty Line of Maharashtra and expenditure distribution of Goa is used to estimate poverty ratio of Goa.

Table A-5

Number and Percentage of Population Below Poverty Line by States, 1983 (Lakdawala Methodology)

S. No.	*States/UTs*	*Rural*		*Urban*		*Total*	
		No. of Persons (Lakhs)	*% of Persons*	*No. of Persons (Lakhs)*	*% of Persons*	*No. of Persons (Lakhs)*	*% of Persons*
1.	Andhra Pradesh	114.34	26.53	50.24	36.30	164.58	28.91
2.	Arunachal Pradesh	2.70	42.60	0.12	21.73	2.82	40.88
3.	Assam	73.43	42.60	4.26	21.73	77.69	40.47
4.	Bihar	417.70	64.37	44.35	47.33	462.05	62.22
5.	Goa	1.16	14.81	1.07	27.00	2.23	18.90
6.	Gujarat	72.88	29.80	45.04	39.14	117.92	32.79
7.	Haryana	22.03	20.56	7.57	24.15	29.60	21.37
8.	Himachal Pradesh	7.07	17.00	0.34	9.43	7.41	16.40
9.	Jammu & Kashmir	13.11	26.04	2.49	17.76	15.60	24.24
10.	Karnataka	100.50	36.33	49.31	42.82	149.81	38.24
11.	Kerala	81.62	39.03	25.15	45.68	106.77	40.42
12.	Madhya Pradesh	215.48	48.90	62.49	53.06	277.97	49.78
13.	Maharashtra	193.75	45.23	97.14	40.26	290.89	43.44
14.	Manipur	4.76	42.60	0.89	21.73	5.65	37.02
15.	Meghalaya	5.04	42.60	0.57	21.73	5.62	38.81

contd...

...contd

16.	Mizoram	1.58	42.60	0.37	21.73	1.96	36.00
17.	Nagaland	3.19	42.60	0.31	21.73	3.50	39.25
18.	Orissa	164.65	67.53	16.66	49.15	181.31	65.29
19.	Punjab	16.79	13.20	11.85	23.79	28.64	16.18
20.	Rajasthan	96.77	33.50	30.06	37.94	126.83	34.46
21.	Sikkim	1.24	42.60	0.10	21.73	1.35	39.71
22.	Tamil Nadu	181.61	53.99	78.46	46.96	260.07	51.66
23.	Tripura	8.35	42.60	0.60	21.73	8.95	40.03
24.	Uttar Pradesh	448.03	46.45	108.71	49.82	556.74	47.07
25.	West Bengal	268.60	63.05	50.09	32.32	318.69	54.85
26.	A & N Island	0.84	53.99	0.26	46.96	1.11	52.13
27.	Chandigarh	0.09	23.79	1.10	23.79	1.19	23.79
28.	Dadra & Nagar Haveli	0.16	14.81	0.02	27.00	0.18	15.67
29.	Delhi	0.44	7.66	17.95	27.89	18.39	26.22
30.							
31.	Pondicherry	1.56	53.99	1.72	46.96	3.28	50.06
	All India	2519.57	45.65	709.40	40.79	3228.97	44.48

Notes: 1. Poverty Ratio of Assam is used for Sikkim, Arunachal Pradesh, Meghalaya, Mizoram, Manipur, Nagaland and Tripura.

2. Poverty Ratio of Tamil Nadu is used for Pondicherry and A & N Island.
3. Poverty Ratio of Kerala is used for Lakshadweep.
4. Poverty Ratio of Goa is used for Dadra & Nagar Haveli.
5. Urban Poverty Ratio of Punjab is used for both rural and urban poverty of Chandigarh.
6. Poverty Line of Maharashtra and expenditure distribution of Goa is used to estimate poverty ratio of Goa.

Table A-6

Number and Percentage of Population Below Poverty Line by States, 1987-88 (Lakdawala Methodology)

S. No.	*States/UTs*	*Rural*		*Urban*		*Total*	
		No. of Persons (Lakhs)	*% of Persons*	*No. of Persons (Lakhs)*	*% of Persons*	*No. of Persons (Lakhs)*	*% of Persons*
1.	Andhra Pradesh	96.38	20.92	64.05	40.11	160.43	25.86
2.	Arunachal Pradesh	2.75	39.35	0.08	9.94	2.83	36.22
3.	Assam	73.53	39.35	2.22	9.94	75.75	36.21
4.	Bihar	370.23	52.63	50.70	48.73	420.93	52.13

5.	Goa	1.31	17.64	1.65	35.48	2.96	24.52
6.	Gujarat	74.13	28.67	48.22	37.26	122.36	31.54
7.	Haryana	18.86	16.22	6.51	17.99	25.37	16.64
8.	Himachal Pradesh	7.27	16.28	0.25	6.29	7.52	15.45
9.	Jammu & Kashmir	14.11	25.70	2.85	17.47	16.95	23.82
10.	Karnataka	96.81	32.82	61.80	48.42	158.61	37.53
11.	Kerala	61.64	29.10	26.84	40.33	88.48	31.79
12.	Madhya Pradesh	200.02	41.92	64.29	47.09	264.30	43.07
13.	Maharashtra	186.89	40.78	109.38	39.78	296.27	40.41
14.	Manipur	4.83	39.35	0.46	9.94	5.29	31.35
15.	Meghalaya	5.18	39.35	0.30	9.94	5.48	33.92
16.	Mizoram	1.46	39.35	0.25	9.94	1.70	27.52
17.	Nagaland	3.49	39.35	0.18	9.94	3.66	34.43
18.	Orissa	149.98	57.64	15.95	41.63	165.93	55.58
19.	Punjab	17.09	12.60	8.08	14.67	25.17	13.20
20.	Rajasthan	104.97	33.21	37.93	41.92	142.90	35.15
21.	Sikkim	1.31	39.35	0.04	9.94	1.36	36.06
22.	Tamil Nadu	161.80	45.80	69.27	38.64	231.07	43.39
23.	Tripura	8.49	39.35	0.35	9.94	8.84	35.23
24.	Uttar Pradesh	429.74	41.10	106.79	42.96	536.53	41.46
25.	West Bengal	223.37	48.30	60.24	35.08	283.61	44.72
26.	Andaman & Nicobar	0.83	45.80	0.26	38.64	1.09	43.89
27.	Chandigarh	0.08	14.67	0.76	14.67	0.84	14.67
28.	Dadra & Nagar Haveli	0.79	67.11	-	-	0.79	67.11
29.	Delhi	0.10	1.29	10.15	13.56	10.25	12.41
30.	Lakshadweep	0.07	29.10	0.10	40.33	0.17	34.95
31.	Pondicherry	1.33	45.80	1.72	38.64	3.05	41.46
	All India	2318.79	39.09	751.69	38.20	3070.49	38.86

Notes: 1. Poverty Ratio of Assam is used for Sikkim, Arunachal Pradesh, Meghalaya, Mizoram, Manipur, Nagaland and Tripura.

2. Poverty Ratio of Tamil Nadu is used for Pondicherry and A & N Island.
3. Poverty Ratio of Kerala is used for Lakshadweep.
4. Urban Poverty Ratio of Punjab used for both rural and urban poverty of Chandigarh.
5. Poverty Line of Maharashtra and expenditure distribution of Goa is used to estimate poverty ratio of Goa.
6. Poverty Line of Maharashtra and expenditure distribution of Dadra & Nagar Haveli is used to estimate poverty ratio of Dadra & Nagar Haveli.

Table A-7

Number and Percentage of Population Below Poverty Line By States, 1993-94 (Lakdawala Methodology)

S. No.	States/UTs	Rural		Urban		Total	
		No. of Persons (Lakhs)	% of Persons	No. of Persons (Lakhs)	% of Persons	No. of Persons (Lakhs)	% of Persons
1.	Andhra Pradesh	79.49	15.92	74.47	38.33	153.97	22.19
2.	Arunachal Pradesh	3.62	45.01	0.11	7.73	3.73	39.35
3.	Assam	94.33	45.01	2.03	7.73	96.36	40.86
4.	Bihar	450.86	58.21	42.49	34.50	493.35	54.96
5.	Goa	0.38	5.34	1.53	27.03	1.91	14.92
6.	Gujarat	62.16	22.18	43.02	27.89	105.19	24.21
7.	Haryana	36.56	28.02	7.31	16.38	43.88	25.05
8.	Himachal Pradesh	15.40	30.34	0.46	9.18	15.86	28.44
9.	Jammu & Kashmir	19.05	30.34	1.86	9.18	20.92	25.17
10.	Karnataka	95.99	29.88	60.46	40.14	156.46	33.16
11.	Kerala	55.95	25.76	20.46	24.55	76.41	25.43
12.	Madhya Pradesh	216.19	40.64	82.33	48.38	298.52	42.52
13.	Maharashtra	193.33	37.93	111.90	35.15	305.22	36.86
14.	Manipur	6.33	45.01	0.47	7.73	6.80	33.78
15.	Meghalaya	7.09	45.01	0.29	7.73	7.38	37.92
16.	Mizoram	1.64	45.01	0.30	7.73	1.94	25.66
17.	Nagaland	4.85	45.01	0.20	7.73	5.05	37.92
18.	Orissa	140.90	49.72	19.70	41.64	160.60	48.56
19.	Punjab	17.76	11.95	7.35	11.35	25.11	11.77
20.	Rajasthan	94.68	26.46	33.82	30.49	128.50	27.41
21.	Sikkim	1.81	45.01	0.03	7.73	1.84	41.43
22.	Tamil Nadu	121.70	32.48	80.40	39.77	202.10	35.03
23.	Tripura	11.41	45.01	0.38	7.73	11.79	39.01
24.	Uttar Pradesh	496.17	42.28	108.28	35.39	604.46	40.85
25.	West Bengal	209.90	40.80	44.66	22.41	254.56	35.66
26.	Andaman & Nicobar	0.73	32.48	0.33	39.77	1.06	34.47
27.	Chandigarh	0.07	11.35	0.73	11.35	0.80	11.35
28.	Dadra & Nagar Haveli	0.72	51.95	0.06	39.93	0.77	50.84
29.	Daman & Diu	0.03	5.34	0.15	27.03	0.18	15.80
30.	Delhi	0.19	1.90	15.32	16.03	15.51	14.69

31.	Lakshadweep	0.06	25.76	0.08	24.55	0.14	25.04
32.	Pondicherry	0.93	32.48	2.38	39.77	3.31	37.40
	All India	2440.31	37.27	763.37	32.36	3203.68	35.97

Notes: 1. Poverty Ratio of Assam is used for Sikkim, Arunachal Pradesh, Meghalaya, Mizoram, Manipur, Nagaland and Tripura.

2. Poverty Ratio of Tamil Nadu is used for Pondicherry and A & N Island.
3. Poverty Ratio of Kerala is used for Lakshadweep.
4. Poverty Ratio of Goa is used for Daman & Diu.
5. Urban Poverty Ratio of Punjab used for both rural and urban poverty of Chandigarh.
6. Poverty Line of Maharashtra and expenditure distribution of Goa is used to estimate poverty ratio of Goa.
7. Poverty Line of Maharashtra and expenditure distribution of Dadra & Nagar Haveli is used to estimate poverty ratio of Dadra & Nagar Haveli.
8. Poverty Ratio of Himachal Pradesh is used for Jammu & Kashmir.

Table A-8

Number and Percentage of Population Below Poverty Line by States, 1999-2000 (Lakdawala Methodology)

S. No.	*States/UTs*	*Rural*		*Urban*		*Total*	
		No. of Persons (Lakhs)	*% of Persons*	*No. of Persons (Lakhs)*	*% of Persons*	*No. of Persons (Lakhs)*	*% of Persons*
1.	Andhra Pradesh	58.13	11.05	60.88	26.63	119.01	15.77
2.	Arunachal Pradesh	3.80	40.04	0.18	7.47	3.98	33.47
3.	Assam	92.17	40.04	2.38	7.47	94.55	36.09
4.	Bihar	376.51	44.30	49.13	32.91	425.64	42.60
5.	Goa	0.11	1.35	0.59	7.52	0.70	4.40
6.	Gujarat	39.80	13.17	28.09	15.59	67.89	14.07
7.	Haryana	11.94	8.27	5.39	9.99	17.34	8.74
8.	Himachal Pradesh	4.84	7.94	0.29	4.63	5.12	7.63
9.	Jammu & Kashmir	2.97	3.97	0.49	1.98	3.46	3.48
10.	Karnataka	59.91	17.38	44.49	25.25	104.40	20.04
11.	Kerala	20.97	9.38	20.07	20.27	41.04	12.72
12.	Madhya Pradesh	217.32	37.06	81.22	38.44	298.54	37.43
13.	Maharashtra	125.12	23.72	102.87	26.81	227.99	25.02
14.	Manipur	6.53	40.04	0.66	7.47	7.19	28.54
15.	Meghalaya	7.89	40.04	0.34	7.47	8.23	33.87
16.	Mizoram	1.40	40.04	0.45	7.47	1.85	19.47
17.	Nagaland	5.21	40.04	0.28	7.47	5.49	32.67
18.	Orissa	143.69	48.01	25.40	42.83	169.09	47.15

contd...

...contd

19.	Punjab	10.20	6.35	4.29	5.75	14.49	6.16
20.	Rajasthan	55.06	13.74	26.78	19.85	81.83	15.28
21.	Sikkim	2.00	40.04	0.04	7.47	2.05	36.55
22.	Tamil Nadu	80.51	20.55	49.97	22.11	130.48	21.12
23.	Tripura	12.53	40.04	0.49	7.47	13.02	34.44
24.	Uttar Pradesh	412.01	31.22	117.88	30.89	529.89	31.15
25.	West Bengal	180.11	31.85	33.38	14.86	213.49	27.02
26.	A & N Island	0.58	20.55	0.24	22.11	0.82	20.99
27.	Chandigarh	0.06	5.75	0.45	5.75	0.51	5.75
28.	Dadra & Nagar Haveli	0.30	17.57	0.03	13.52	0.33	17.14
29.	Daman & Diu	0.01	1.35	0.05	7.52	0.06	4.44
30.	Delhi	0.07	0.40	11.42	9.42	11.49	8.23
31.	Lakshadweep	0.03	9.38	0.08	20.27	0.11	15.60
32.	Pondicherry	0.64	20.55	1.77	22.11	2.41	21.67
	All India	1932.43	27.09	670.07	23.62	2602.50	26.10

Notes:
1. Poverty Ratio of Assam is used for Sikkim, Arunachal Pradesh, Meghalaya, Mizoram, Manipur, Nagaland and Tripura.
2. Poverty Line of Maharashtra and expenditure distribution of Goa is used to estimate poverty ratio of Goa.
3. Poverty Line of Himachal Pradesh and expenditure distribution of Jammu & Kashmir is used to estimate poverty ratio of Jammu & Kashmir.
4. Poverty Ratio of Tamil Nadu is used for Pondicherry and A & N Island.
5. Urban Poverty Ratio of Punjab used for both rural and urban poverty of Chandigarh.
6. Poverty Line of Maharashtra and expenditure distribution of Dadra & Nagar Haveli is used to estimate poverty ratio of Dadra & Nagar Haveli.
7. Poverty Ratio of Goa is used for Daman & Diu.
8. Poverty Ratio of Kerala is used for Lakshadweep.

Table A-9

Number and Percentage of Population Below Poverty Line By States, 2004-05 (Lakdawala Methodology)

S. No.	*States/UTs*	*Rural*		*Urban*		*Total*	
		No. of Persons (Lakhs)	*% of Persons*	*No. of Persons (Lakhs)*	*% of Persons*	*No. of Persons (Lakhs)*	*% of Persons*
1.	Andhra Pradesh	64.70	11.2	61.40	28.0	126.10	15.8
2.	Arunachal Pradesh	1.94	22.3	0.09	3.3	2.03	17.6
3.	Assam	54.50	22.3	1.28	3.3	55.77	19.7
4.	Bihar	336.72	42.1	32.42	34.6	369.15	41.4
5.	Chhattisgarh	71.50	40.8	19.47	41.2	90.96	40.9

6.	Delhi	0.63	6.9	22.30	15.2	22.93	14.7
7.	Goa	0.36	5.4	1.64	21.3	2.01	13.8
8.	Gujarat	63.49	19.1	27.19	13.0	90.69	16.8
9.	Haryana	21.49	13.6	10.60	15.1	32.10	14.0
10.	Himachal Pradesh	6.14	10.7	0.22	3.4	6.36	10.0
11.	Jammu & Kashmir	3.66	4.6	2.19	7.9	5.85	5.4
12.	Jharkhand	103.19	46.3	13.20	20.2	116.39	40.3
13.	Karnataka	75.05	20.8	63.83	32.6	138.89	25.0
14.	Kerala	32.43	13.2	17.17	20.2	49.60	15.0
15.	Madhya Pradesh	175.65	36.9	74.03	42.1	249.68	38.3
16.	Maharashtra	171.13	29.6	146.25	32.2	317.38	30.7
17.	Manipur	3.76	22.3	0.20	3.3	3.95	17.3
18.	Meghalaya	4.36	22.3	0.16	3.3	4.52	18.5
19.	Mizoram	1.02	22.3	0.16	3.3	1.18	12.6
20.	Nagaland	3.87	22.3	0.12	3.3	3.99	19.0
21.	Orissa	151.75	46.8	26.74	44.3	178.49	46.4
22.	Punjab	15.12	9.1	6.50	7.1	21.63	8.4
23.	Rajasthan	87.38	18.7	47.51	32.9	134.89	22.1
24.	Sikkim	1.12	22.3	0.02	3.3	1.14	20.1
25.	Tamil Nadu	76.50	22.8	69.13	22.2	145.62	22.5
26.	Tripura	6.18	22.3	0.20	3.3	6.38	18.9
27.	Uttar Pradesh	473.00	33.4	117.03	30.6	590.03	32.8
28.	Uttarakhand	27.11	40.8	8.85	36.5	35.96	39.6
29.	West Bengal	173.22	28.6	35.14	14.8	208.36	24.7
30.	A & N Islands	0.60	22.9	0.32	22.2	0.92	22.6
31.	Chandigarh	0.08	7.1	0.67	7.1	0.74	7.1
32.	Dadra & N. Haveli	0.68	39.8	0.15	19.1	0.84	33.2
33.	Daman & Diu	0.07	5.4	0.14	21.2	0.21	10.5
34.	Lakshadweep	0.06	13.3	0.06	20.2	0.11	16.0
35.	Pondicherry	0.78	22.9	1.59	22.2	2.37	22.4
	All-India	2209.24	28.3	807.96	25.7	3017.20	27.5

Notes:
1. Poverty Ratio of Assam is used for Sikkim, Arunachal Pradesh, Meghalaya, Mizoram, Manipur, Nagaland and Tripura.
2. Poverty Line of Maharashtra and expenditure distribution of Goa is used to estimate poverty ratio of Goa.
3. Poverty Ratio of Tamil Nadu is used for Pondicherry and A & N Island.
4. Urban Poverty Ratio of Punjab used for both rural and urban poverty of Chandigarh.
5. Poverty Line of Maharashtra and expenditure distribution of Dadra & Nagar Haveli is used to estimate poverty ratio of Dadra & Nagar Haveli.
6. Poverty Ratio of Goa is used for Daman & Diu.

Annexure–B

Table B-1

State-specific Poverty Lines (Tendulkar Methodology)

(₹ per capita per month)

S. No.	*States*	*Rural*			*Urban*		
		2004-05	*2009-10*	*2011-12*	*2004-05*	*2009-10*	*2011-12*
1.	Andhra Pradesh	433	694	860	563	926	1009
2.	Arunachal Pradesh	547	774	930	618	925	1060
3.	Assam	478	692	828	600	871	1008
4.	Bihar	433	656	778	526	775	923
5.	Chhattisgarh	399	617	738	514	807	849
6.	Delhi	541	748	1145	642	1040	1134
7.	Goa	609	931	1090	671	1025	1134
8.	Gujarat	502	726	932	659	951	1152
9.	Haryana	529	792	1015	626	975	1169
10.	Himachal Pradesh	520	708	913	606	888	1064
11.	Jammu & Kashmir	522	723	891	603	845	988
12.	Jharkhand	405	616	748	531	831	974
13.	Karnataka	418	629	902	588	908	1089
14.	Kerala	537	775	1018	585	831	987
15.	Madhya Pradesh	408	632	771	532	772	897
16.	Maharashtra	485	744	967	632	961	1126
17.	Manipur	578	871	1118	641	955	1170
18.	Meghalaya	503	687	888	746	990	1154
19.	Mizoram	639	850	1066	700	939	1155
20.	Nagaland	687	1017	1270	783	1148	1302
21.	Odisha	408	567	695	497	736	861
22.	Punjab	544	830	1054	643	961	1155
23.	Rajasthan	478	755	905	568	846	1002
24.	Sikkim	532	729	930	742	1035	1226
25.	Tamil Nadu	442	639	880	560	801	937
26.	Tripura	450	663	798	556	783	920
27.	Uttar Pradesh	435	664	768	532	800	941
28.	Uttarakhand	486	720	880	602	899	1082
29.	West Bengal	445	643	783	573	831	981
30.	Puducherry	385	641	1301	506	778	1309
	All India	447	673	816	579	860	1000

Table B-2

Number and Percentage of Population Below Poverty Line by States, 2004-05 (Tendulkar Methodology)

S. No.	*States/UTs*	*Rural*		*Urban*		*Total*	
		No. of Persons (Lakhs)	*% of Persons*	*No. of Persons (Lakhs)*	*% of Persons*	*No. of Persons (Lakhs)*	*% of Persons*
1.	Andhra Pradesh	32.3	187.1	23.4	51.3	29.9	238.8
2.	Arunachal Pradesh	33.6	2.9	23.5	0.7	31.1	3.6
3.	Assam	36.4	88.8	21.8	8.4	34.4	97.3
4.	Bihar	55.7	445.1	43.7	40.9	54.4	485.6
5.	Chhattisgarh	55.1	96.5	28.4	13.4	49.4	109.9
6.	Delhi	15.6	1.4	12.9	18.9	13.1	20.4
7.	Goa	28.1	1.9	22.2	1.7	25.0	3.6
8.	Gujarat	39.1	130.1	20.1	41.9	31.8	172.2
9.	Haryana	24.8	39.3	22.4	15.8	24.1	55.1
10.	Himachal Pradesh	25.0	14.3	4.6	0.3	22.9	14.6
11.	Jammu & Kashmir	14.1	11.3	10.4	2.9	13.2	14.2
12.	Jharkhand	51.6	115.1	23.8	15.6	45.3	130.7
13.	Karnataka	37.5	135.0	25.9	50.8	33.4	185.7
14.	Kerala	20.2	49.5	18.4	15.7	19.7	65.0
15.	Madhya Pradesh	53.6	255.3	35.1	61.7	48.6	316.9
16.	Maharashtra	47.9	277.1	25.6	116.1	38.1	393.3
17.	Manipur	39.3	6.6	34.5	2.1	38.0	8.7
18.	Meghalaya	14.0	2.7	24.7	1.2	16.1	3.9
19.	Mizoram	23.0	1.1	7.9	0.4	15.3	1.4
20.	Nagaland	10.0	1.7	4.3	0.2	9.0	1.9
21.	Orissa	60.8	197.3	37.6	22.7	57.2	220.2
22.	Puducherry	22.9	0.8	9.9	0.7	14.1	1.5
23.	Punjab	22.1	36.5	18.7	17.2	20.9	53.8
24.	Rajasthan	35.8	167.2	29.7	42.8	34.4	210.3
25.	Sikkim	31.8	1.6	25.9	0.2	31.1	1.8
26.	Tamil Nadu	37.5	125.6	19.7	61.3	28.9	186.8
27.	Tripura	44.5	12.3	22.5	1.3	40.6	13.7
28.	Uttar Pradesh	42.7	604.7	34.1	130.3	40.9	735.5
29.	Uttarakhand	35.1	23.3	26.2	6.4	32.7	29.7
30.	West Bengal	38.2	231.2	24.4	57.9	34.3	289.1
	All India	41.8	3266.6	25.7	807.6	37.2	4076.1

Notes: Population as on 1st March 2005 has been used for estimating number of persons below poverty line. (Revised on the basis of 2011 population census)

Table B-3

Number and Percentage of Population Below Poverty Line by States, 2009-10 (Tendulkar Methodology)

S. No.	States/UTs	Rural		Urban		Total	
		No. of Persons (Lakhs)	% of Persons	No. of Persons (Lakhs)	% of Persons	No. of Persons (Lakhs)	% of Persons
1	Andhra Pradesh	22.8	127.9	17.7	48.7	21.1	176.6
2	Arunachal Pradesh	26.2	2.7	24.9	0.8	25.9	3.5
3	Assam	39.9	105.3	26.1	11.2	37.9	116.4
4	Bihar	55.3	498.7	39.4	44.8	53.5	543.5
5	Chhattisgarh	56.1	108.3	23.8	13.6	48.7	121.9
6	Delhi	7.7	0.3	14.4	22.9	14.2	23.3
7	Goa	11.5	0.6	6.9	0.6	8.7	1.3
8	Gujarat	26.7	91.6	17.9	44.6	23.0	136.2
9	Haryana	18.6	30.4	23.0	19.6	20.1	50.0
10	Himachal Pradesh	9.1	5.6	12.6	0.9	9.5	6.4
11	Jammu & Kashmir	8.1	7.3	12.8	4.2	9.4	11.5
12	Jharkhand	41.6	102.2	31.1	24.0	39.1	126.2
13	Karnataka	26.1	97.4	19.6	44.9	23.6	142.3
14	Kerala	12.0	21.6	12.1	18.0	12.0	39.6
15	Madhya Pradesh	42.0	216.9	22.9	44.9	36.7	261.8
16	Maharashtra	29.5	179.8	18.3	90.9	24.5	270.8
17	Manipur	47.4	8.8	46.4	3.7	47.1	12.5
18	Meghalaya	15.3	3.5	24.1	1.4	17.1	4.9
19	Mizoram	31.1	1.6	11.5	0.6	21.1	2.3
20	Nagaland	19.3	2.8	25.0	1.4	20.9	4.1
21	Orissa	39.2	135.5	25.9	17.7	37.0	153.2
22	Puducherry	0.2	0.01	1.6	0.1	1.2	0.1
23	Punjab	14.6	25.1	18.1	18.4	15.9	43.5
24	Rajasthan	26.4	133.8	19.9	33.2	24.8	167.0
25	Sikkim	15.5	0.7	5.0	0.1	13.1	0.8
26	Tamil Nadu	21.2	78.3	12.8	43.5	17.1	121.8
27	Tripura	19.8	5.4	10.0	0.9	17.4	6.3
28	Uttar Pradesh	39.4	600.6	31.7	137.3	37.7	737.9
29	Uttarakhand	14.9	10.3	25.2	7.5	18.0	17.9

30	West Bengal	28.8	177.8	22.0	62.5	26.7	240.3
31	Andaman & Nicobar Island	0.4	0.01	0.3	0.004	0.4	0.01
32	Chandigarh	10.3	0.03	9.2	0.9	9.2	1.0
33	Dadra and Nagar	55.9	1.0	17.7	0.3	39.1	1.3
34	Daman and Diu	34.2	0.2	33.0	0.5	33.3	0.8
35	Lakshadweep	22.2	0.03	1.7	0.01	6.8	0.04
	All India	33.8	2782.1	20.9	764.7	29.8	3546.8

Notes: 1. Population as on 1st March 2010 has been used for estimating number of persons below poverty line. (interpolated between 2001 and 2011 population census)

2. Poverty line of Tamil Nadu is used for Andaman and Nicobar Island.
3. Urban Poverty Line of Punjab is used for both rural and urban areas of Chandigarh.
4. Poverty Line of Maharashtra is used for Dadra & Nagar Haveli
5. Poverty line of Goa is used for Daman & Diu.
6. Poverty Line of Kerala is used for Lakshadweep.

Table B-4

Number and Percentage of Population Below Poverty Line by States, 2011-12 (Tendulkar Methodology)

S. No.	*States/UTs*	*Rural*		*Urban*		*Total*	
		No. of Persons (Lakhs)	*% of Persons*	*No. of Persons (Lakhs)*	*% of Persons*	*No. of Persons (Lakhs)*	*% of Persons*
1	Andhra Pradesh	11.0	61.8	5.8	17.0	9.2	78.8
2	Arunachal Pradesh	38.9	4.2	20.3	0.7	34.7	4.9
3	Assam	33.9	92.1	20.5	9.2	32.0	101.3
4	Bihar	34.1	320.4	31.2	37.8	33.7	358.2
5	Chhattisgarh	44.6	88.9	24.8	15.2	39.9	104.1
6	Delhi	12.9	0.5	9.8	16.5	9.9	17.0
7	Goa	6.8	0.4	4.1	0.4	5.1	0.8
8	Gujarat	21.5	75.4	10.1	26.9	16.6	102.2
9	Haryana	11.6	19.4	10.3	9.4	11.2	28.8
10	Himachal Pradesh	8.5	5.3	4.3	0.3	8.1	5.6
11	Jammu & Kashmir	11.5	10.7	7.2	2.5	10.3	13.3
12	Jharkhand	40.8	104.1	24.8	20.2	37.0	124.3
13	Karnataka	24.5	92.8	15.3	37.0	20.9	129.8
14	Kerala	9.1	15.5	5.0	8.5	7.1	23.9

contd...

...contd

15	Madhya Pradesh	35.7	191.0	21.0	43.1	31.6	234.1
16	Maharashtra	24.2	150.6	9.1	47.4	17.4	197.9
17	Manipur	38.8	7.4	32.6	2.8	36.9	10.2
18	Meghalaya	12.5	3.0	9.3	0.6	11.9	3.6
19	Mizoram	35.4	1.9	6.4	0.4	20.4	2.3
20	Nagaland	19.9	2.8	16.5	1.0	18.9	3.8
21	Orissa	35.7	126.1	17.3	12.4	32.6	138.5
22	Punjab	7.7	13.4	9.2	9.8	8.3	23.2
23	Rajasthan	16.1	84.2	10.7	18.7	14.7	102.9
24	Sikkim	9.9	0.4	3.7	0.1	8.2	0.5
25	Tamil Nadu	15.8	59.2	6.5	23.4	11.3	82.6
26	Tripura	16.5	4.5	7.4	0.8	14.0	5.2
27	Uttar Pradesh	30.4	479.4	26.1	118.8	29.4	598.2
28	Uttarakhand	11.6	8.2	10.5	3.4	11.3	11.6
29	West Bengal	22.5	141.1	14.7	43.8	20.0	185.0
30	Puducherry	17.1	0.7	6.3	0.6	9.7	1.2
31	A & N Islands	1.6	0.04	0.0	0.0	1.0	0.04
32	Chandigarh	1.6	0.004	22.3	2.3	21.8	2.3
33	Dadra & Nagar Haveli	62.6	1.2	15.4	0.3	39.3	1.4
34	Daman & Diu	0.0	0.0	12.6	0.3	9.9	0.3
35	Lakshadweep	0.0	0.0	3.4	0.02	2.8	0.02
	All India	25.7	2166.6	13.7	531.2	21.9	2697.8

Notes: 1. Population as on 1st March 2012 has been used for estimating number of persons below poverty line. (2011 Census population extrapolated)

2. Poverty line of Tamil Nadu is used for Andaman and Nicobar Island.
3. Urban Poverty Line of Punjab is used for both rural and urban areas of Chandigarh.
4. Poverty Line of Maharashtra is used for Dadra & Nagar Haveli
5. Poverty line of Goa is used for Daman & Diu.
6. Poverty Line of Kerala is used for Lakshadweep.

3

Issues in Poverty Estimation

Our review in Chapter 2 of the methodology of estimating the number and proportion of poor people in the country recommended by earlier expert groups—from the 1979 Task Force (Alagh) through Export Group (Lakdawala) and including Expert Group (Tendulkar)—has highlighted a few key issues which need to be resolved before we proceed to spell out the methodology recommended by this (Rangarajan) Expert Group.

Poverty Line Basket or PLB: All-India or State-Specific baskets

The first question is of the use of a single all-India poverty line (or, rather, a poverty line basket or PLB) to derive state—specific, rural-urban basket of goods and services the access (or, otherwise) to which separates the poor from the non-poor. This becomes crucial in a continental-sized country such as ours that is marked by significant variability in living environment (including, but not limited to, climatic conditions), in dietary patterns and preferences and, in prices of goods and services across states and as between rural and urban areas even within the same state. This issue was explicitly raised by Mr. S. Guhan (Member, Export Group (Lakdawala) in the context of both, the practice followed by the Planning Commission on the adoption of the recommendations of the 1979 Task Force (Alagh) as well as the recommendations of the Expert Group (Lakdawala).

On a careful consideration of this issue, the Expert Group (Lakdawala) came to the conclusion that, having decided to accept the minimum living standard for defining poverty line normatively, "it should be applied uniformly to all parts of the country for assessing poverty. The commodity basket corresponding to this norm should be standardised at the national level and applied to all States. This is being recommended in order to enable comparability across states and overtime" (GoI, 1993: 31). This view was also implicitly endorsed by the Expert Group (Tendulkar).

The practice followed by the Planning Commission on the acceptance of the recommendations of the 1979 Task Force (Alagh) and Expert Group (Lakdawala), up to and until the adoption of the recommendations of the Expert Group (Tendulkar), has been to work with two separate poverty line baskets for the rural and urban areas at the all India level and deriving State-specific poverty cut-offs by adjustments for price-differentials. On a view that "Urban living standard is generally regarded as better than and preferable to its rural counterpart", the Expert Group (Tendulkar) recommended that the purchasing power represented by the MRP-equivalent PCTE (MPCE) underlying the all-India (urban) HCR of 25.7 per cent be taken as the new reference PLB for measuring poverty and made available to both the rural and urban population in all the states after correcting for urban-rural price differentials as well as urban and rural state-relative-to-all-India price differentials" (GoI, 2009: 7).

The Expert Group (Rangarajan) proposes to revert back to the earlier practice of having separate all India poverty line baskets for rural and urban areas by reference to which the state-level & rural and urban poverty lines will be derived.

Income or Consumption Expenditure

It would be clear from the common reference to poverty line basket of goods and services in the methodologies of the 1979 Task Force (Alagh) and the Lakdawala and Tendulkar Expert Groups that the underlying metric of living standards is consumption expenditure rather than incomes of the households. This conscious decision follows from the significant difficulties of capturing household incomes through recall-based (typically with a 30-day reference period) surveys canvased over a moving sample of households.

These difficulties are particularly sizeable in the case of households with self-employment as the principal source of income. In the case of such households, the flow of incomes may be staccato—at the time of harvests in the case of agriculture, uneven over the year (as in trading) or uncertain (in agriculture). Also, these households may be drawing incomes from more than one enterprise where a major proportion of these enterprises do not maintain full accounts/

balance-sheets. Consequently, even in the absence of will-full under-reporting of incomes, there are serious problems in capturing the incomes of self-employed households. As per the NSS 68th Round (2011-12) survey, self-employed households form 49.8 per cent of all households in rural India and 35.3 per cent per cent of all urban households.

In the case of households dependent on wage employment getting a measure of their wage incomes is possible from the NSS Employment-Unemployment Surveys. Even in this case, however, households dependent on casual wage labour (accounting for 34.5 per cent of rural households and 11.8 per cent of urban households) face considerable intra—year variability in income flows from casual labour since they are not assured of employment through the year. This problem is absent in the case of households having regular wage/ salaries employment as their principal source of income. However, even in the case of these households, problems of capturing their incomes from their non-labour assets remain.

If estimating wage incomes from employment surveys pose the above noted problems, capturing both income and expenditure of the households pose even greater difficulties. These have been brought out clearly by the NSS Pilot survey on Income and Expenditure. Given the length and the complex nature of the survey schedules for the Consumer Expenditure and Employment Unemployment Surveys, there are serious concerns about respondent fatigue affecting the quality of responses and the resulting non-sampling errors. This has prompted the NSSO to discontinue, after the 50th Round (1993-94), canvassing both schedules from the same sample households. They are now canvassed over a different set of sample households drawn from the same universe.

Notwithstanding these problems, the CMIE has carried out a very interesting exercise in locating the poor households by reference to their ability or otherwise to have at the least a small margin of saving by way of excess of their incomes over their consumption expenditure. This provides valuable insights into the dynamic processes underlying poverty in India and hence is included in this Report (see Annexure 4.1).

Nutrition Norms, Nutrition Content of Food Basket and Nutrition Outcomes:

Post the acceptance of the report of the 1979 Task Force (Alagh), the calorie norms developed by the Task Force became the basis of the official all India PLB, separately for the rural and urban populations, and their price-adjusted monetary equivalents became the state-level poverty lines on the recommendations of the Expert Group (Lakdawala). However, Expert Group (Tendulkar) consciously moved away using calorie norms to derive the all India PLB", In view of the fact that calorie consumption calculated by converting the consumed quantities (of food) in the last 30-days as collected by NSS has not been found to be well correlated with the nutrition outcomes observed from other specialized surveys either over time or across space (i.e. between states or rural and urban areas)" (GoI, 2009: 1). This position merits a very careful review.

Our first comment is a re-iteration of a point clearly spelt out by Expert Group (Lakdawala). We quote, "This way of deriving the poverty line (linked to the calorie norms), while being anchored in a norm of calorie requirement, does not seek to measure the nutritional status, and more specifically the incidence of malnourishment or under-nourishment" (GoI, 1993: 5).

Second, over time there have been significant shifts in consumption patterns (Table 4). We have a sizeable reduction in the share of food in total expenditure, and, within food, a significant reduction in the share of calorie-rich cereals.

Even the composition of cereal consumption shows a shift from coarse cereals to the more expensive source of calories—rice and wheat. Broadly speaking, there has been a shift away from a calorie-intensive diet towards a more diversified food basket richer in proteins and fats. This shift has occurred across expenditure classes. As has been noted by Deaton and Dreze (2009), these shifts in consumption patterns could be reflective of lower calorie requirements following the changes in occupational patterns towards a more sedentary life style, improvements in access to better sanitation and hygiene and general improvements in health status leading to better retention of ingested calories and other nutrients.

Table 4

Percentage Share in Consumer Expenditure

	Item Groups	Rural				
		1993-94	1999-2000	2004-05	2009-10	2011-12
1.	Share of Cereals, gram & Cereal subs in Food Total	38.8	37.7	33.1	29.7	25.3
2.	Share of Pulses, milk, edible oil, Eggs, Meat & fish, Veg and fruits in Food Total	45.4	46.3	50.0	50.9	54.1
3.	Share of Other Food in Food Total	15.8	16.2	17.1	19.4	20.6
4.	Share of Food in Total Consumption	63.2	59.4	55.0	53.6	48.6
5.	Share of Non-Food in Total Consumption	36.8	40.6	45.0	46.4	51.4
		Urban				
1.	Share of Cereals, gram & Cereal subs in Food Total	26.1	26.0	24.0	22.6	19.5
2.	Share of Pulses, milk, edible oil, Eggs, Meat & fish, Veg and fruits in Food Total	52.7	52.4	53.9	54.5	54.8
3.	Share of Other Food in Food Total	21.2	21.2	22.1	22.9	26.0
4.	Share of Food in Total Consumption	54.7	48.1	42.5	40.7	38.5
5.	Share of Non-Food in Total Consumption	45.3	51.9	57.5	59.3	61.5

Note: Based on URP estimates except for 1999 200, for which only MRP estimates are available.

Source: NSS Report No. 555 (68/1.0/1), February 2014.

This Expert Group (Rangarajan) has re-computed the average requirements of calories, fats and proteins on the basis of the 2010 ICMR norms; the age and gender distribution of the rural and urban populations as per the 2011 Population Census; and, the broad work status distribution as per the 2011-12 Employment Unemployment Survey. The revised calorie norms are indeed lower—especially in rural India (see chapter 4 of the Report).

Third, assessing the presence or absence of correlation between the calorie content of the average quantity of food consumed in 2011-12 and nutrition status outcomes poses several problems:

(a) the most- recent results of a nationwide survey on the nutrition status of children and adults relate to 2005-06 (NFHS-3). Clearly, there is an urgent need for more current data on the nutrition status of the population and updates on the same at regular intervals. This Expert Group (Rangarajan) strongly recommends a regular programme of NFHS or NFHS-type nationwide surveys.; and,

(b) in carrying out an assessment of the relationship between the calorie-content of current food consumption and nutrition-status outcomes, we need to segregate the nutrition-status outcomes of children from that for the adults

A recent paper by Meenakshi and Viswanathan (Meenakshi and Viswanathan, 2013) shows that, with the elimination of a few outliers, adult BMI outcomes (as per NFHS 3 results) and calorie-intake (or, rather the calorie-content of the food items consumed) are indeed correlated. However, the same is not true in respect of nutrition-status outcomes for children.

In interpreting this, and other similar, results in respect of the correlation between calorie-intakes and nutrition-status indicators for children, it needs to be stressed that in all these studies there are no controls for other significant determinants of nutrition-status of children such as availability, access and utilisation of vaccination and immunization services by mother and child during the pre and post-natal periods. A recent paper by Bhargava et al (Bhargava et al., 2011) brings out the statistically significant impact of these factors on different facets of child nutrition status. Another interesting result reported by Bhargava et al. is that a rise in the index of diversity of food consumed (in terms of number of different food-groups such as cereals, pulses, vegetables, milk, eggs, etc. consumed per day) has a statistically significant impact on anaemia among children. Seen in this light, the shift in consumption patterns observed across expenditure classes towards a more diversified diet would, ceteris paribus, have a favourable impact on child nutrition outcomes. More recently, Coffey, Deaton, Dreze, Spears and Tarozzi (2013) have highlighted the role of what they call the "disease environment" in shaping anthropometric outcomes of children in India. Controlling for all these factors, we can reasonably expect a statistically significant contribution of intakes of nutrient intakes (including but not limited to Calories) to nutrition outcomes of children in India.

It is the assessment of this Expert Group (Rangarajan) that a food basket that successfully meets the newly worked out nutrition norms in terms of calories and of proteins and fats is an essential pre-requisite for satisfactory nutrition-status outcomes. Here it is important to see the calorie norm as a range rather than a single number. As the Expert Group (Lakdawala) pointedly notes", differences in energy requirements due to climatic variations, the role of inter- and intra-individual differences in the efficiency of utilisation of food intake and variations in food preferences have to be explicitly taken into account" (GoI 1993: 31). It also draws attention to the divergence of opinion among experts "on (a) the validity of prescribing a unique calorie norm for a given age/sex/occupation category and (b) the margin within which individuals can adapt, without adverse impact on health or activity status, to variations in intake around the norm" (Ibid).

It is also the assessment of this Expert Group (Rangarajan) that, when taken in conjunction with the full range of policies and programmes for child nutrition support and other initiatives in the area of vaccination and immunization for mother and child and of committed delivery by the Government of essential public goods and services (such as sanitation, hygiene and safe drinking water) that shape what Coffey et al. call the disease environment, the normative food basket defined above does offer a basis for optimism on associated nutrition-status outcomes. Needless to say, these nutrition-status outcomes will materialise with a lag rather than contemporaneously.

Comparison of NSS and NAS Estimates of Household Consumption Expenditure

Like most of the countries, Indian statistical system is endowed with two parallel estimates of private consumption. These are:

(a) NSS estimates, which comes from the household consumer expenditure survey and yields class distribution of consumption by sectors (rural and urban) and by regions (states, and sub-state level such as NSS regions, which are formed by grouping contiguous districts similar in density of population and cropping pattern).

(b) NAS estimates, originating from the CSO. It yields a scalar value of consumption for the nation as a whole, with no disaggregation by region or class (except by broad commodity groups).

These two estimates of consumption (NSS and NAS) do not match in any country; India is no exception. What is alarming in India is that the difference between the NSS and the NAS consumption is widening overtime. For example, the difference was less than 10 per cent in the late 1970s; it rose to 50 per cent in 2004-05. At the aggregate level, the NAS consumption has always been more than the NSS consumption.

Since the NAS consumption is greater than the NSS consumption, and if the latter is raised pro-rata by region and expenditure groups of the population, the poverty ratio after such adjustment would turn out to be lower than what would have been estimated from the NSS consumption data without such adjustment.

The Task Force (Alagh) recommended the adjustment of NSS consumption to the levels of NAS consumption at the national level to estimate poverty. It was necessary for using poverty as a parameter in the medium- and long-term consistency plan models. To ensure that the macro-economic variables used in the plan model are consistent, the consumption used there has to be from the NAS. Also, the NSS and NAS consumption did not differ much in those days. The difference between the then two as mentioned above was less than 10 per cent.

Using the Task Force (Alagh) methodology, the Planning Commission estimated poverty after adjusting the NSS consumption distribution (obtained from the consumer expenditure survey) in regions such as rural and urban, and within each region between different States and Union Territories and for each of these by the different expenditure groups of the population, pro-rata by the difference between the two consumption estimates, i.e., the NAS and the NSS.

The Planning Commission gave up the adjustment of the NSS consumption following the recommendations of the Expert Group (Lakdawala) in March 1997. When the Expert Group (Lakdawala) took this decision, the difference between the NSS and NAS consumption touched forty per cent. This made the methodology of poverty estimation by the Planning Commission relying exclusively on the NSS consumption. Subsequently, the Expert Group (Tendulkar) also relied exclusively on the NSS consumption to estimate poverty. The present methodology of poverty estimation by the Planning Commission therefore, does not take cognisance of the NAS consumption and relies exclusively on the NSS consumption.

As will be clear from the above, this issue is not new. It has again gained salience due to a widening of the gap between the two estimates and an examination of "the issue of divergence between consumption estimates based on the NSSO methodology and those emerging from the National Accounts aggregates" is an explicit part of the TOR for this Expert Group (Rangarajan). The divergence between NSS and NAS estimates of private consumption expenditure from 1972-73 to 2009-10 is given in Table 5.

A number of studies have been conducted in the past by academicians, (Minhas (1988); Minhas and Kansal (1989), and Sundaram and Tendulkar (2003) to cite a few), and, by officials of the National Accounts Division of the CSO, MoSPI. Reviewing the studies by Minhas et al., Expert Group (Lakdawala) came to the considered judgement that "it is indeed hazardous to carry out pro-rata adjustment in the size distribution of consumer expenditure in a particular NSS round by multiplying it with a scalar derived from the ratio between the NAS estimate of the aggregate private consumption for the nearest financial year and the total NSS expenditure available from that particular NSS round" (GoI 1993: 12)

Table 5

Divergence between the NSS and NAS Estimates of Private Consumption Expenditure

(₹ crores)

Year	*Source*	*Food*	*Non-food*	*Total*
1972-73	NSS	23420	9790	33210
(1970-71 base)	NAS	23379	11752	35131
% difference of NSS from NAS		0.18	-16.7	-5.47
1977-78	NSS	36500	20030	56530
(1970-71 base)	NAS	39801	23282	63083
% difference of NSS from NAS		-8.29	-13.97	-10.39
1983-84	NSS	69735	39996	109731
(1980-81 base)	NAS	85613	60471	146084
% difference of NSS from NAS		-18.55	-33.86	-24.88
1987-88	NSS	106205	67560	173765
(1980-81 base)	NAS	122805	101256	224061
% difference of NSS from NAS		-13.52	-33.28	-22.45
1993-94	NSS	224066	131704	355770
(1993-94 base)	NAS	315243	259529	574772
% difference of NSS from NAS		-28.92	-49.25	-38.1
1999-2000	NSS	393126	323265	716391
(1993-94 base)	NAS	652627	618929	1271556
% difference of NSS from NAS		-39.76	-47.77	-43.66
1999-00	NSS	410918	305473	716391
(1999-00 base)	NAS	647011	610530	1257541
% difference of NSS from NAS		-36.49	-49.97	-43.03
2004-05 (URP)	NSS	481189	450226	931415
(1999-00 base)	NAS	742609	1131120	1873729
% difference of NSS from NAS		-35.2	-60.2	-50.29
2004-05 (MRP)	NSS	481189	485204	966393
(1999-00 base)	NAS	742609	1131120	1873729
% difference of NSS from NAS		-35.2	-57.1	-48.42
2004-05 (URP)	NSS	481189	450226	931415
(2004-05 base)	NAS	769500	1156092	1925592
% difference of NSS from NAS		-37.5	-61.1	-51.63

2004-05 (MRP)	NSS	481189	485204	966393
(2004-05 base)	NAS	769500	1156092	1925592
% difference of NSS from NAS		-37.5	-58.0	-49.81
2009-10 (URP sch type 1)	NSS	835316	1011890	1847206
(2004-05 base)	NAS	1372064	2423837	3795901
% difference of NSS from NAS		-39.1	-58.3	-51.34
2009-10 (MRP sch type 1)	NSS	760162	1142154	1902316
(2004-05 base)	NAS	1372064	2423837	3795901
% difference of NSS from NAS		-44.6	-52.9	-49.88
2009-10 (MMRP sch type 2)	NSS	1017817	1040111	2057928
(2004-05 base)	NAS	1372064	2423837	3795901
% difference of NSS from NAS		-25.8	-57.1	-45.8

The Expert Group (Lakdawala) also drew attention to the need for adjusting for differences in:

i) Coverage (NAS estimates include the expenditure incurred by Non-Profit Institutions Serving Households (NPISH) on goods and services provided to households as social transfers in kind which do not form part of consumption expenditure by households captured by NSS surveys);

ii) Time-periods with July-June agricultural production taken as the output base for NAS estimates for the financial year April-May. If there are significant differences in agricultural output in the April-June quarter of two successive years, this would affect the NAS-NSS comparison;

iii) Classification schemes used in the two sets of estimates; and,

iv) Implicit-prices underlying the two set of estimates.

In articulating its reasoning for preferring the use of NSS estimates without any scalar adjustments over the NAS estimates, the Expert Group (Lakdawala) noted that:

> The NAS estimate of private consumption is derived as a residual by deducting from estimated production of the various goods and services (adjusted for foreign trade the estimated use for capital formation and public consumption. Apart from lack of reliable direct data on production for a sizeable segment of the economy, the adjustments for uses other than private consumption are based on scanty data, often of the distant past and subjective judgements.... (GoI, 1993: 13).

A few points on the above are in order. First, a recent (November 2013) meeting of the Committee on Private Final Expenditure (under the Chairmanship of Prof A.K. Adhikari) set up by the National Accounts Advisory Committee notes as follows: "The Committee looked into the existing rates and ratios being used in estimation of PFCE in agriculture, manufacturing and service sectors commodities. It noted that many rates and ratios in use are quite old".

Finally, an exercise that adjusts agricultural produce for the Financial Year and uses updated IO rates including Trade Transport margins and taxes reduces the difference between the NAS and NSS estimates for 2009-10 from 25.8 per cent to 23.3 per cent for food; from 57.1 to 52.2 per cent for non-food and from 45.8 per cent to 41.2 per cent in the aggregate (Table 6).

Table 6

Divergence between the NSS and NAS Estimates of Consumption Expenditure After Adjustments (₹ Crore)

Year	*Source*	*Food*	*Non-food*	*Total*
2009-10 (MMRP sch type 2)	NSS-unadjusted	1017817	1040111	2057928
(2004-05 base)	NAS-unadjusted	1372064	2423837	3795901
% difference		-25.8	-57.1	-45.8
2009-10 (MMRP sch type 2)	NSS-unadjusted	1017817	1040111	2057928
	NAS-Adjusted	1327745	2174669	3502414
% difference		-23.3	-52.2	-41.2
2009-10(MMRP sch type 2)	NSS-adjusted	1017817	1347621	2365438
	NAS-Adjusted	1327745	2174669	3502414
% difference		-23.3	-38.0	-32.5

There is one other major adjustment in the NAS estimates that needs to be made for valid comparisons between these estimates and the NSS based estimates. In respect of non-food expenditure the Financial Intermediation Services Indirectly Measures (FISIM), Life Insurance Premium (together totalling 131844 crores) and Imputed Gross Rental (over 175666 crores) are part of NAS estimates with no counterpart estimates in NSS Consumer Expenditure Surveys. An adjustment for this factor reduces the divergence between these two estimates from 52.2 per cent to 38.0 per cent for non-food and from 41.2 per cent to 32.5 per cent overall.

This order of divergence between the two sets of estimates is still very large and deserves further scrutiny. In respect of expenditure on Food, analysis at the item-group level shows that NSS-estimates are higher for Pulses and Products, Edible Oils and Non-Alcoholic Beverages (Tea). Four item-groups—Sugar and Gur; Milk and Milk Products; Meat, Eggs and Fish; Fruits and Vegetables-taken together account for more than the total excess of NAS-over-NSS estimates for Food as a group.

Sugar and Gur has always been problematic. Apart from non-recorded cross-border exports (see Minhas et al reference earlier), rates and ratios being used for feed, marketed surplus, wastage, etc. in the case of Gur has been flagged for review by the Adhikari Committee (2013). The same is true for 'Fish Curing' and for Fish, Inland and Marine.

Currently, in NSS Consumer Expenditure surveys, even as the expenditures on Meat, Egg and Fish, Edible Oils and Fruits and Vegetables are canvassed on a 7-day reference period, expenditure on Milk and Milk Products continue to be canvassed on a 30-day reference period. This issue needs to be re-visited in the experimental designs now under consideration.

In respect of non-food expenditures, education, sports and athletics goods and recreation and cultural services, as well as, fuel, show an excess of NSS-estimates over their NAS counterparts. The case of education (and culture and recreation) is interesting from two perspectives.

First, as per the findings of a recent survey of Non-Profit Institutions, the total output of NPIs (included as part of NAS-estimates) measured nearly 23 per cent of the NAS-estimate of PFCE in education and 79 per cent of NAS–estimate of PFCE in Culture and Recreation. Adjusting for this would make the excess of NSS estimates over their NAS counterparts even larger.

Secondly, a comparative analysis of per capita expenditure education emerging from the NSS 64th Round (2007-08) Survey on Education and from the traditional Consumer Expenditure Survey for the same 64th Round, shows that the former estimates are significantly higher. An upward adjustment of the NSS estimates for expenditure on education on this account would further increase the excess of these estimates over their NAS counterpart

The NAS estimates for medical care and health services are based on projections based on note health accounts based on the NSS 60th Round focused survey on expenses on health care—rather than current estimates for the later years. It needs to be noted that included in the NAS estimates of PFCE in healthcare are expenditures by non-household players such as Insurance companies and ESI etc.

The case of education and medical and health services points to an urgent need for specialized Surveys by NSSO covering the full range of publicly provided services under the rubric of Social Consumption Surveys. This Expert Group recommends periodic social consumption surveys-preferably, in very close proximity to the Consumer Expenditure Surveys.

Significant contributors to the sizeable excess of the NAS over the NSS-estimates include Furniture, Furnishings, Appliances and Transport Equipment and Operational Cost and Transport Services—chiefly, under the rubric "Bus Including Tramways". From the perspective of measurement of poverty, the impact of possible inadequate capture of expenditures on transport equipment and operational cost in the NSS survey may be expected to be less than of inadequate capture in NSS surveys of the expenditure on "Bus Including Tramways". In many of these cases of NAS-estimates of non-food expenditures significantly exceeding the corresponding NSS–estimates this may be reflective of possible non-sampling errors arising from the fact that the expenditures are canvassed towards the end of a very long schedule. Experiments with alternative designs of CES need to be carried out urgently.

The above analysis has shown that:

i) A part of the divergence between the NSS and the NAS estimates is purely notional in that the latter includes consumption by NPISH, FISIM, and Imputed Rentals on owner-occupied dwellings for which there can be no NSS-counterpart;

ii) At the item-group-level, the differences are bi-directional; and,

iii) There are infirmities in both sets of estimates.

In view of the foregoing, this Expert Group (Rangarajan) will continue with the current practice—initiated by the Expert Group (Lakdawala) and continued by the Expert Group (Tendulkar)—of estimating poverty in India solely by reference to the size-distribution of private consumer expenditure based on the NSSO methodology.

Adjusting Poverty Lines for Spatial and Inter-temporal Variations in Prices: Evolution of the Methodology

In implementing the 1979 Task Force (Alagh), the Planning Commission used a single common all-India poverty line for all the States—albeit separate ones for the Rural and the Urban populations. For adjusting the all-India poverty lines for price-inflation over time the Wholesale Price Index (WPI, for short) was used to adjust both the rural and the urban poverty lines. This posed the obvious problem that the WPI had a substantial weightage for items that were not of the consumption basket of the households. Subsequently, the Planning Commission used the implicit deflator underlying the current and the constant price values of PFCE in the National Accounts. This, too, did not provide separate indicators for the rural and the urban populations.

The Expert Group (Lakdawala) made some key changes. First, using State-relative-to-all-India Fisher Price Indices computed by Chatterji and Bhattacharya (1974) for Rural areas and the Minhas et al. (1988) estimates for urban India, State-specific poverty lines corresponding to the Task Force all-India poverty lines were derived. Secondly, State-specific poverty lines were up-dated by reference to re-weighted Consumer Price Indices—of Agricultural labourers for rural areas and of Industrial workers for urban areas). This re-weighting raised the weightage of the FOOD COMPONENT OF THE RELEVANT INDICES to correspond to the share of food in the consumption basket of those around the poverty line at the all-India level. Finally, the price-updated all-India Poverty lines were derived indirectly by reference to the population-weighted average of the State-level poverty ratios and the all-India size-distribution of Consumer Expenditure.

The changes in consumption patterns discussed earlier posed two sets of problems for the Expert Group (Lakdawala) methodology outlined above (See Deaton, 2008). First, the reduction in the share of cereals in total food expenditure to levels well-below those implicit in the Food component of the Consumer price indices affected the ability of the price index to capture food inflation adequately when prices of non-cereal food items rose faster than Cereal prices. Second, the fall in the share of Food in total consumption to levels significantly below the elevated weightage assigned in the Expert Group (Lakdawala) methodology, implied that the true inflation faced by those around the poverty line may be higher(lower) depending on whether non-food inflation was higher (lower) than food inflation .

In the face of changing consumption patterns, any Consumer Price Index with fixed base-year weights, will not be able to capture the true inflation faced by the population. Recognising this, the Expert Group (Tendulkar) decided to work with Fisher price indices specifically estimated both for deriving State-specific poverty lines given the all-India (Urban) poverty line and for updating the same over time. The procedure for deriving the price-updated all-India poverty lines—given the updated State-specific poverty lines—remained the same as that in the Expert Group (Lakdawala) methodology. The underlying price-relatives were provided by a combination of Unit Values emerging from the NSS Consumer Expenditure Surveys and the price-relatives underlying the available Consumer Price Indices. While the weighting diagrams for the State vs all-India exercise was provided by the average budget shares of the rural (urban) populations of the State under reference and all-India. For the inter-temporal State-specific Fisher Indices, the weighting diagrams for the base and the terminal years were provided by the consumption patterns of the rural (urban) populations around the (State-specific) poverty lines.

The implications of the above review of the methodology for adjusting for price-differences across space and price-inflation time for adjusting the poverty lines developed by this Expert Group (Rangarajan) will be taken up in Chapter 4.

Public Expenditure on Social Services and Their Impact on Poverty

In the seven-year period 2004-05 to 2011-12, public expenditures on Education and Health per capita at constant 2004-05 prices have nearly doubled with an implied CAGR of close to 10 per cent per annum (Table 7). Given that these services are, typically, provided at heavily subsidised prices—if not given free, the reported private expenditures as captured in the NSS Consumer Expenditure Surveys on them would be lower than their true value. To that extent, this component of the Poverty Line Basket will carry a lower monetary value relative to the true value of these services to the households at that threshold. However, in the absence of data on the distribution of the public expenditures on these Social Services by size-class of private consumption expenditure, they can-not be factored into either the construction of the poverty line or in the assessment of their impact on measured poverty.

Parenthetically, we may note that, in terms of lowering the true value of private consumption expenditure, access by households to PDS has an impact similar to that of access of households to subsidized services in education and health. However, in the case of PDS, we do have information on the MPCE of households using PDS and the quantities of grains etc. bought. One could, therefore, analyse the impact of PDS on Measured poverty (Himanshu and Abhijit Sen)

Table 7

Per Capita Per Month Public Expenditure at Constant Prices (2004-05)

Year	*Education*	*Health*
2004-05	78	20
2005-06	90	25
2006-07	85	26
2007-08	95	27
2008-09	101	28
2009-10	129	32
2010-11	146	36
2011-12	157	38

Methodology of Poverty Estimation in Other Countries

The Expert Group (Rangarajan) deliberated on the methodology of poverty estimation employed in other countries, both developing and developed. Most of the developing countries use consumption basket linked to balanced diet as the poverty cut-off point. Developed countries generally use the concept of relative poverty and in some countries the poverty line is defined as an exogenously set proportion of mean or median income of the population.

The concept of relative poverty is more readily applicable to economies where the average levels of living are high and when it is applied by reference to incomes which exhibit greater inequality than consumer expenditure. As can be seen from Table 8 and Table 9, the proportion of population with consumption as a pre-determined fraction of the median remains largely invariant over time.

Table 8

Percentage of Persons Below Different Levels of Median Per Capita Consumer Expenditure in Rural Areas

		2004-05 (NSS 61st Round)	*2009-10 (NSS 66th Round)*	*2011-12 (NSS 68th Round)*
1.	0.5 of Median	3.5	3.9	4.2
2.	0.6 of Median	9.4	10.1	10.4
3.	0.7 of Median	18.6	19.0	19.4
4.	0.8 of Median	29.4	29.3	29.9
5.	0.9 of Median	40.0	40.0	40.4
6.	1.0 of Median	50.0	50.0	50.0
7.	1.1 of Median	58.6	58.7	57.9
8.	1.2 of Median	65.8	66.0	64.8
9.	1.3 of Median	72.0	71.9	70.7

N.B.: The estimates are derived from MRP-consumption distribution.

It is however possible to define the absolute poverty line basket of goods and services, or components thereof, by reference to the consumption pattern of households located in the median expenditure class. The same can also be done by reference to any MPCE-class defined as a fraction of the median expenditure. For estimating poverty in other years, of course, the reference to the median (or a fraction thereof) is purely incidental and only the chosen Poverty Line Basket remains relevant.

Table 9

Percentage of Persons Below Different Levels of Median Per Capita Consumer Expenditure in Urban Areas

		2004-05 (NSS 61st Round)	2009-10 (NSS 66th Round)	2011-12 (NSS 68th Round)
1.	0.5 of Median	9.6	10.4	10.9
2.	0.6 of Median	18.1	18.9	18.9
3.	0.7 of Median	26.7	27.9	27.4
4.	0.8 of Median	35.4	35.9	35.6
5.	0.9 of Median	43.1	43.2	43.2
6.	1.0 of Median	50.0	50.0	50.0
7.	1.1 of Median	55.7	55.9	56.3
8.	1.2 of Median	60.8	60.7	61.6
9.	1.3 of Median	65.7	65.2	66.4

N.B.: Same as in Table 8.

Poverty Estimates by the World Bank

The World Bank estimates the incidence of poverty in its member countries at regular intervals. The approach of poverty estimation by the World Bank is similar to those employed in India and in most of the developing countries. The World Bank estimates of poverty are based on the poverty line of US $1.25 per person per day measured at 2005 international price and adjusted to local currency using PPP (purchasing power parity) conversion factor computed in the World Bank. The international poverty line is worked out as the average of national poverty lines in poorest 15 countries (in terms of consumption per capita) using 2005 ICP (International Comparison Programme) data.

The poverty estimates made by the World Bank are based on same poverty line for all its member countries. In contrast, the Planning Commission methodology uses state-specific and also region-specific (rural and urban) poverty lines. Therefore, these poverty lines capture the regional prices more precisely. The methodology of poverty estimation by the World Bank does not allow for cost of living differential within countries and it also does not distinguish between transient and chronic poverty, which is critical in devising the strategy for poverty alleviation, particularly in the low income developing countries. In terms of the latest set of PPP-values (World Bank, 2014), the national poverty line of the Planning Commission for 2011-12, after adjusting it to Indian currency using PPP conversion factor is $ 1.94 a day.

Reviewing the method of estimation of poverty in other countries, the Expert Group (Rangarajan) arrived at the conclusion that neither their methodological nor procedural aspects are superior to what is being used in India at present. The estimates of poverty in India are based on a methodology which stands far apart for it is able to measure the incidence of poverty by capturing the demographic pattern and consumer behaviour separately in rural and urban areas and also by capturing the state-wise variation in the prices of goods and services.

Non-Income Dimension of Poverty

The very first of the Terms of Reference (TOR) for this Expert Group (Rangarajan) requires the Group to examine, inter-alia "whether the poverty line should be fixed solely in terms of consumption basket or whether other criteria are also relevant and, if so, whether the two can be effectively combined to evolve a basis for estimation of poverty, rural and urban areas."

The search for "other criteria" possibly stems from a view that, in terms of the capabilities approach to the concept and measurement of poverty, some of these 'capabilities', or, rather, the lack thereof may not be tightly linked to the privately purchased consumption basket in terms of which the poverty lines are currently drawn. A few such key capabilities are; (i) to be (at least minimally) educated; (ii) to escape avoidable diseases; and (iii) to be adequately sheltered.

In the area of education, for example, the observed outcome, in terms of, say, the proportion of illiterates in the adult population, would primarily reflect the cumulative impact of past provisioning of public services and private decisions to avail of these services and to utilise a part of private purchasing power for the same and for essential complementary goods and services. Even as we accept this position, it is important to stress that current expenditure on education, both, private and public are extremely important as they do shape the educational outcomes for today's children. A reasonable provisioning for this in our definition of poverty line is an important first step.

In respect of the capability to "escape avoidable diseases', morbidity and mortality may be expected to be more closely associated with availability and access to safe drinking water, sewage and sanitation facilities rather than the money value of the privately purchased consumption basket. Similarly, the capability to be adequately sheltered will be defined by the key characteristics of housing structures and housing amenities which may be weakly correlated (if at all) with levels of private consumption expenditure.

Seen from the 'capability' perspective outlined above, the elements of "other criteria" would, perhaps, be an amalgam of some outcome indicators in the area of education and health: input indicators for a range of public goods and services; and some characteristics of housing structures and amenities. These are also listed as components of a so-called "Multi-dimensional" measure of poverty (See for example a recent paper by OPHDI).

These Indicators/Measures raise several issues regarding their measurability, aggregation across indicators, and, crucially, of data bases that provide the requisite information at reasonably short intervals. These need to be considered and evaluated carefully.

As regards measurability, mortality indicators, as probabilistic measure are appropriately defined only for population groups rather for individual households (seen from this perspective, the child mortality indicator used in the OPHDI-study does appear to be problematic). As for morbidity, self-reported episodes of illness captured by NSS Morbidity Surveys could be seriously misleading and out of alignment with mortality indicators for the same population group.

Consider next the issue of aggregation. To be aggregable, in principle, the indicators must be independent of one another: access to safe drinking water, for example, cannot be aggregated with indicators, of, say, child mortality. Second, even in respect of independent indicators, analytically appropriate rules of aggregation require that all of them relate to the same household. It is this factor that dictated the choice of NFHS-3 (2005-06) as the data base for OPHDI-study, which, in turn, dictated the choice of the indicators used in the study. This would hardly be appropriate for an index for the present day. More generally, this requirement poses several data constraints. For example, Decennial Censuses provide valuable information on access of households to a range of housing amenities—water, electricity—and about the materials used for the floor, the walls and the roof of structures that house the population. Besides the obvious issues of periodicity (once in 10 years), this information cannot be combined with those from NSS surveys on social consumption (on access to publicly provided good and services) or the NSS Employment-Unemployment Surveys that capture school attendance of children and educational outcome for all.

Most importantly, the fact that the data sources listed above, and, the same holds good for the data collected under the SECC-2011 as well, cannot be combined with the Consumer Expenditure surveys—the data base for poverty line defined in terms of consumption basket-as they relate to different sets of household, also rules out combining it with indicators based on "other Criteria" as proposed in the TOR.

Poverty Ratio for Eligibility and Entitlements Under Poverty Alleviation Programmes

At present, substantial amount of investment of the Department of Rural Development, which are meant for income generation of the poor do not go through the BPL regimentation. In fact, as much as 92 per cent of the funds flowing to the rural areas through the of Department of Rural Development do not require the BPL list since these programmes are no longer exclusively for the poor, and are universalized. For example, the wage employment programme

Mahatma Gandhi National Rural Employment Guarantee Act (MGNREGA), by far the single most important programme for the poor is not exclusively for the poor; it is universalized. The MGNREGA do not need a BPL list since both the poor and the non-poor access the employment equally.

Till last year, TPDS was one of the important programmes linked to poverty ratio. Now, the Government has embarked on a large-scale food security programme for its citizens by bringing in two-third of the country's population (three-fourth of the rural population and half of the urban population) under its cover. In both rural and urban areas, therefore, poverty is no longer the criterion to access food from the public distribution system. But, the food security programme makes it imperative to draw up a list of households, from which it could be possible to identify the bottom 75 per cent of the rural households and bottom 50 per cent of the urban households. Therefore, BPL list in some form retain not only its relevance, but seem to gain in importance due to the supply of highly subsidized food grains to ensure food security.

The National Rural Livelihood Mission (NRLM), which is a self-employment programme for rural poor, Indira Awas Yojana (IAY), the housing programme in rural areas and National Old Age Pension Scheme (NOAPS), a welfare programme for rural poor are the three programmes that remain target-group oriented (i.e. for the poor only) and require the BPL list. But, these programmes have other criteria for selection of beneficiaries. For example, homelessness is used as a criterion to select and prioritise the poor families in IAY. NRLM is a self-help group movement based scheme. NOAPS has other pre-requisites such as minimum age.

The Expert Group (Rangarajan) deliberated on the issue of use of poverty ratio for determining the eligibility and entitlements for a wide range of poverty alleviation programmes and social welfare schemes implemented by various Ministries and Departments of the Government of India in association with the State Governments.

The Group recommends that the beneficiaries under target group oriented schemes of the Government may be selected from the deprivation-specific ranking of households. Such ranking of households could be generated for a large number of indicators representing deprivation and levels of living for which the information has been gathered at the household and individual level in the SECC-2011and population census. The beneficiaries could be selected from this set of households until the resources earmarked for the programme/scheme permit. Poverty ratio of Planning Commission can play an important role in deciding allocation of resources among States. The Ministries and Departments in association with the State Governments may draw the guidelines for defining the beneficiaries for their programmes. The process could be similar in rural and urban areas.

4

The Suggested Methodology for Measurement of Poverty

Real incomes and real consumption have grown at a significantly faster pace between 2004-05 and 2011-12 than during any comparable period since the early 1950's. Over this period, aggregate GDP and per capita GDP (both at constant 2004-05 prices) grew at an annual average rate of 8.5 and 6.9 per cent. Also over this period, real private per capita consumption grew at a compound Annual Growth Rate of 2.9 and 3.4 per cent, respectively, in rural and urban India. Along-side, significant changes have occurred in the composition of private consumption expenditure: a reduction in the share of food, of food grains within food and of cereals within food grains.

It is against this background that this Expert Group (Rangarajan) has to define its methodology for drawing up the poverty line and the measurement of poverty. This involves determining the poverty line basket of goods and services and the associated level of monthly per capita (total) private consumption expenditure as captured by the NSS Consumer Expenditure Surveys. Prior to that, we need to resolve the issue of choice among three alternative reference (recall) periods for which the NSS Surveys provide estimates of private consumption expenditure.

Choice of Recall Period

Three estimates of consumption along with its regional and class distribution are presently available from the NSSO depending upon the recall (reference) period of data collection. These are: (a) Uniform Recall Period (URP), (b) Mixed Recall Period (MRP) since 1993-94, and (c) Modified Mixed Recall Period (MMRP) for 2009-10 and 2011-12.

In the URP, the consumption expenditure data are collected using 30-day recall period for all the items.

In the MRP, the consumption expenditure data are collected using 365-day recall period for five non-food items and 30-day recall period for remaining items.

In the MMRP, the consumer expenditure data is gathered from the households using the recall period of: (a) 365-days for clothing, footwear, education, institutional medical care, and durable goods, (b) 7-days for edible oil, egg, fish and meat, vegetables, fruits, spices, beverages, refreshments, processed food, pan, tobacco and intoxicants, and (c) 30-days for the remaining food items, fuel and light, miscellaneous goods and services including non-institutional medical; rents and taxes.

Experts are of the view that the mix of reference periods for different items underlying the MMRP -estimates may be expected to yield estimates that are closer to their "true value" (See, NSSO Expert Group on Non-Sampling Errors in Deaton & Kozel, 2005). Our discussions in Chapter 3 on the divergence between the NAS and the NSS estimates of private consumer expenditure also showed that the differences between the two estimates were lower with NSS estimates based on MMRP. Further, in all future NSS Consumer Expenditure Surveys only the MMRP estimates will be available.

All three factors listed above made the choice of recall periods in favour of MMRP by the Expert Group (Rangarajan) both obvious and inevitable despite the fact that it automatically implies that deriving poverty estimates using MMRP distribution is not possible for all years prior to 2009-10.

The New Poverty Line Basket

In defining the new consumption basket separating the poor from the rest, the Expert Group (Rangarajan) is of the considered view that it should contain a food component that addresses the capability to be adequately nourished as well as some normative level of consumption expenditure for essential non-food item groups (Education, clothing, conveyance and house rent) besides a residual set of behaviorally determined non-food expenditure.

As a first step towards defining the food component of the poverty line basket, the Expert Group (Rangarajan) has recomputed the average requirements of calories, proteins and fats, per capita per day at the all-India level for 2011-12, separately for the rural and the urban populations. This has been done by reference to the 2010 ICMR norms differentiated by age, gender and activity-status; the age and gender distribution of All-India rural and urban populations as per the 2011 Population Census; and, the broad work-status distribution, again by age and gender and separately for the rural and urban population, as per the NSS 68th Round Employment–Unemployment Survey (2011-12).

The Revised Norms for Calories, Proteins and Fats

The calorie norms based on which the Task Force (Alagh) poverty lines were derived, and which had been the basis for the poverty lines worked out by the Expert Group (Lakdawala), is 2400 kcal per capita per day in rural areas and 2100 kcal per capita per day in urban areas.

The calorie norm for each category of the population in terms of age, sex and activity is lower as per the 2010 ICMR norms relative to those recommended by the Nutrition Expert Group (1968). For example, the calorie norm of male workers engaged in heavy activities was 3900 kcal per capita per day in the late 1960s (based on which the Task Force estimated the calorie norms for the all-India rural and urban populations).[11] The latest ICMR norm (2010) for this group is 3490 kcal which is 410 kcal per person per day lower.

The activity structure of population has also changed in such a manner that the proportion of population in the activity–categories requiring relatively higher calorie intake is now lower. The proportion of population engaged as heavy workers has reduced overtime, while that of moderate or sedentary workers has increased. This lowers the average calorie norm of the entire population because calorie requirement of moderate or sedentary workers is much less than that of heavy workers. For example, in case of male workers, the requirement per capita per day is: 3490 kcal for persons engaged in heavy work, 2730 kcal for persons engaged in moderate work and 2320 kcal for persons engaged in sedentary work; for female workers, the calorie requirement is: 2850/2230/1900 kcal per capita per day in heavy/moderate/sedentary work.

---

11. The Task Force (1979) used the calorie norms of ICMR which were based on the recommendations of the Nutrition Expert Group, 1968.

Table 10

Average Calorie Requirement

Age-Sex-Occupation Categories			*Popul. Wts as per 2011-12 EUS/Census 2011*		*ICMR-norm 2010*		
			Rural	*Urban*	*calorie*	*Protein*	*Fat*
less than 1			1.79	1.44	585	10.2	19
1-3			6.07	4.83	1060	16.7	27
4-6			6.70	5.19	1350	20.1	25
7-9			6.65	5.24	1690	29.5	30
10-12			7.33	5.85	2100	40.0	35
13-14	Male		2.22	1.92	2750	54.3	45
	Female		2.06	1.76	2330	51.9	40
15 -59	Male	Sedentary	3.67	13.66	2320	60.0	25
		Moderate	12.78	9.03	2730	60.0	30
		Heavy	7.93	3.84	3490	60.0	40
		Non-worker	5.35	7.31	2320	60.0	25
	Female	Sedentary	1.05	3.43	1900	55.0	20
		Moderate	5.45	1.64	2230	55.0	25
		Heavy	4.03	1.53	2850	55.0	30
		Non-worker	17.78	24.84	1900	55.0	20
60 & above	Male	Sedentary/ non-worker	4.32	4.00	2320	60.0	25
	Female		4.47	4.11	1900	55.0	20
Calorie requirement			2154.91	2089.35			
Protein requirement			48.17	50.08			
Fat requirement			27.61	25.88			

Note: These refer to non-pregnant non-lactating women only. To the extent that some women in 15-49 age group would be pregnant and therefore require more calories, the average norms would be marginally higher, but declining over time as the total fertility rate falls. This aspect is not captured here.

Faced with a situation of lowering of the calorie norms of each age-sex-activity group of the population and an altered population distribution which is biased in favour of the occupations requiring relatively lower calories, an exercise has been carried out (similar to that carried out by the 1979 Task Force) to calculate the average calorie requirement in rural and urban areas.

Using the latest estimate of the age-sex-activity specific calorie norm as recommended by the ICMR (2010); the population weighting diagram derived from the 2011Population Census 2011; and the age-gender location-specific work-status categories from the NSS 68th round NSS Employment-Unemployment Survey (2011-12), average calorie requirements have been worked out separately for the all-India rural and urban populations. This is given in Table 10. The average calorie requirement works out to 2155 kcal per capita per day in rural areas and 2090 kcal per capita per day in urban areas. It is readily seen that for rural India, these revised calorie norms for 2011-12 are substantially lower than those derived by the Task Force (Alagh). In the case of urban areas, however, due to a more pronounced shift in the age-distribution towards adults with higher calorie requirements, the revised calorie norm for the urban population is only marginally lower than those derived by the Task Force (Alagh).

In rural areas, the lowering of the estimated calorie norm from the Task Force (from 2400 kcal to 2155 kcal per capita per day, i.e. by 245 kcal per capita per day) is the outcome of change in the population structure and the overall lowering of the average age-sex-activity-specific calorie requirement of the individuals as determined by the ICMR. The first factor, i.e. the change in the population structure is a part of the emerging demographic pattern concomitant with the overall rate of growth of the economy. The second factor, i.e. the overall lowering of the calorie requirement of the individuals owes to the changes in the lifestyle of all sections of the society (Deaton and Dreze (2009). It is possible to decompose the lowering of the calorie norm into these two factors. It is observed that lowering of the age-sex-activity specific calorie norm of the ICMR is responsible for 60 per cent of the reduction in the calorie requirement of the population between 1979 and 2011. The remaining 40 per cent of the reduction in the calorie requirement is due to a change in the structure of the population during the period.

A couple of points on the revised calorie norms are in order.

i. First, as a recent study by Meenakshi and Viswanathan shows, the average calorie norms could be significantly lower if we replace the 95th Per centile heights and a BMI of 21 that underline the ICMR norms for adults by a possibly more appropriate (for the current adult population whose height is given) median (or mean) heights and a BMI of 19 that is still higher than the lower limit of 18.5 that defines a healthy adult.
ii. Secondly, we have the idea (Sukhatme, 1982) of a margin of homeostatic adaptation within which individuals can adapt, without adverse impact on health and activity status, to variation in intakes around the norms.

These two factors would suggest that the calorie norms be treated as lying in range, of, say, ±10 per cent, where intakes at the lower level need not compromise their health and activity status.

Two other factors are also relevant in shaping our assessment of adequacy or otherwise of the measured calorie-content of the food items bought/consumed relative to the desired calorie norm.

i. First, there are inter and intra-individual differences in the efficiency of utilization of food intake.
ii. Secondly, the standard measurement of nutrient-content of food consumption from NSS Consumer Expenditure Surveys do not account for meals received outside either as wages, or, free (as in the case of free mid-day meals for children). A proper meal-accounting exercise, typically, raises the estimated calorie-intakes—especially in the lower fractile—groups.

Similar to the calculations made for calorie requirement, protein and fat requirements have been estimated using age-sex-activity specific protein and fat norms recommended by the ICMR in 2010 and population weighting diagram of 2011. The average protein and fat requirement works out to be 48 gms and 28 gms per capita per day in rural areas. In urban areas, the average protein and fat requirement works out to be 50 gms and 26 gms per capita per day.

A food basket that simultaneously meets all the norms for the three nutrients, with the calorie-norm being satisfied at least at the lower level of the range defines the food component of the poverty line basket proposed by the Expert Group (Rangarajan). In thus anchoring the food component of the poverty line basket, the Expert Group (Rangarajan) takes the considered position that, taken in conjunction with public policies for full nutrition support for children in the 0-6 age-group and public provisioning of a range of public goods and services (Sanitation, drainage, drinking water and immunization and vaccination etc.) on a universal basis[12], the access to the food component of the PLB will have a favourable impact on the nutrition-status outcomes for the population. Simultaneously, the Expert Group (Rangarajan) recognizes that such favourable outcomes may come about with a lag rather than being observed contemporaneously.

The latest information on class distribution of nutrient-intake, based on estimates of food consumption on MMRP, is available for the year 2011-12 (NSS 68th Round). It is seen that the nutrient-intake norms, including the calorie–norms at the lower end of the range, are met for the persons located in the sixth fractile (25-30%) in rural areas and for those in the fourth fractile (15-20%) in urban areas. The average monthly per capita consumption expenditure on food in these fractile classes is ₹554 in rural areas and ₹656 in urban areas.

Deriving the Non-Food Component of the Poverty Line Basket (PLB)

The non-food component of the PLB has both a normative component and, a component given by the observed consumption pattern of households in the fractile-group in which the food

12. The importance of public provisioning on a universal basis of public goods and services listed above extends beyond conditioning the anthropometric outcomes of children to conditioning the probability of a member of a household falling ill by influencing what Coffey et.al call the " disease environment". A reduced probability of illness, will, in turn, reduce the private expenditure on health care that is contingent on that eventuality. If, additionally, we have in place a publicly-funded universal health insurance scheme supported by appropriate health care infrastructure, it will substantially reduce the requirements for private expenditure needed to escape avoidable disease.

component of the PLB is located. The normative component relates to the private consumption expenditure aimed at capabilities in respect of education, clothing, shelter (rent) and mobility (conveyance). Since it is difficult to set minimum norms for these essential non-food items, the Expert Group (Rangarajan) recommends that observed expenditures on these items by households located in the median fractile (45-50 percentile) be treated as the normative minimum private consumption expenditure on these items. For all other non-food goods and services, the observed expenditure of that fractile-class which meets the nutrient-norms (the 25th-30th per centile in rural India, and, the 15th-20th per centile in urban India) is taken to define the PLB in respect of these items.

The monthly per capita consumption expenditure which constitutes new poverty line basket, separately in rural and urban areas, is given below in Table 11.

Table 11

Consumption Expenditure of PLB in Rural Areas and Urban Areas-2011-12 (MPCE in ₹)

Items	*Rural*		*Urban*	
	Sixth fractile (25-35%)	*Median class (45-50%)*	*fourth fractile (15-20%)*	*Median class (45-50%)*
Food	554	678	656	977
Four essential non-food items	102	141	181	407
Other non-food items	277	347	344	571
Total MPCE	933	1166	1181	1955
MPCE-Poverty Line	972		1407	

The Monthly Per-capita Consumption Expenditure (MPCE) of ₹972 (554+141+277) in rural areas and ₹1,407 (656+407+344) in urban areas constitute the new poverty lines at the all- India level as per the recommendation of the Expert Group (Rangarajan). They translate to a monthly per household expenditure of ₹4,860 in Rural India and of ₹7,035 for urban India—assuming a family of 5-members in each case.

Seen in relation to the Median Expenditure of the all-India rural and urban populations (₹1,191 and ₹2,009 respectively), the poverty-line level of monthly per capita private consumption expenditure (MPCE) proposed by the Expert Group (Rangarajan) is seen to be 82 per cent of the median expenditure for Rural India, and, 70 per cent of the median expenditure for Urban India.

Seen in terms of the share of non-food expenditure in the PLB, it is 43 per cent in rural areas and 53 per cent in urban areas. The share of different items in poverty line basket, separately for rural and urban areas is given in Annexure C-1.

Finally, we can see the proposed poverty line level MPCE in terms of PPP dollars per capita per day. As per the most recent (World Bank, 2014) PPP–values, the PLB-MPCE translates to $ 2.14 per capita per day for Rural India, $ 3.10 per capita per day for Urban India and $ 2.44 per capita per day for the country as a whole. (In PPP conversion US $1= ₹15.11) An Alternate Empirical Estimation of the Poverty Line Converges with the Normative Estimation

Estimations obtained from a completely different survey of households and by a completely different methodology yield results that are remarkably close to the ones obtained above using the NSSO data. The study finds the poverty line in terms of monthly per capita consumption expenditure at ₹1,010 in rural areas and ₹1,282 in urban areas. These estimates are 3.9 per cent and 8.9 per cent per cent apart from the estimates based on the NSSO's data. The closeness of these two independent and large systems of locating the poverty line lends an additional support to the estimations made by the Expert Group (Rangarajan).

The alternate survey was conducted by the Centre for Monitoring Indian Economy. CMIE conducts a survey on a panel of about 150,000 households every quarter to collect data on household income and consumption expenses, besides other information. Household income and expenses data for the year 2011-12 was derived as the sum of the quarterly income and expenses observed in the four surveys conducted on the entire panel during the year.

The poverty line, in this study, is defined as a maximum level of household income at which a household is unable to meet its consumption expenses. A household is considered poor if it is unable to save. And, the value of income (or expenses) at which households are unable to save is defined to be the poverty line. The poverty line in this methodology is therefore derived entirely from the observed data of household income and expenses. It is not dependent upon any assumptions or norms regarding a minimum standard of living. A detailed not on the study is presented in Annexure C-2.

Increase in the Poverty Line

The existing Official Planning Commission poverty lines for 2011-12, based on Expert Group (Tendulkar) methodology and derived from the Mixed Recall Period (MRP) consumption distribution of the NSSO, are ₹816 and ₹1,000 per capita per month, for, respectively, the all-India Rural and Urban populations. The Expert Group (Rangarajan) poverty lines, based on consumption estimates on MMRP are, thus 19 per cent higher for Rural India and 41 per cent higher for Urban India. Because of the differences in the underlying recall periods, only a part of the total difference (₹156 for rural India & ₹407 in urban India) between the current official poverty lines and those proposed by the Expert Group (Rangarajan) is real. To see this, note that, a rural Head Count Ratio of 30.9 per cent with a poverty line MPCE of ₹972 on the MMRP consumption distribution will translate to ₹868 on the MRP size-distribution. Similarly, in the case of urban India the poverty line of ₹1,407 (and, the associated HCR of 26.4 per cent) on MMRP will translate to a MPCE of ₹1,293 on MRP. So that, 67 per cent (972-868/156) and 28 per cent (1,407-1,293/407) of the two sets of poverty lines for rural and urban India, respectively, will merely reflect the change in the underlying recall periods, and, in that sense, notional. The balance of the difference between the two sets of poverty lines (₹52 for the rural and ₹293 for the urban areas) represents what may be termed as the real increase in the poverty lines flowing from the recommendations of the Expert Group (Rangarajan).

Some further comments on the differences between the current official poverty lines and the ones proposed by the Expert Group (Rangarajan) are in order. First, not only is the size of the difference between the two sets of poverty lines larger in urban India (₹407 or 41 per cent vs ₹156 and 19 per cent in Rural India, in the Urban case, the Food/non-food composition is heavily weighted (67 per cent) in favour of non-food expenditures. And, of this difference in non-food expenditures, the four selected non-food items for which the Expert Group (Rangarajan) has recommended normative levels of expenditure, together, account for an overwhelming 91 per cent. Further, of this difference due to these 4 items, Conveyance and house rent account for over 50 per cent. The fact that in rural India only a small proportion of households reside in hired dwellings requiring payment of rent shows up in average rents of less than ₹1 per month even in the median fractile is an important part of the explanation for the smaller absolute difference as between the two sets of Rural poverty lines. In the case of rural India, in contrast, the differences in respect of food expenditures in the two sets of poverty lines account for 65 per cent of the total and, of this again, nearly 74 per cent is accounted for by the shift from MRP to MMRP.

From a different perspective, the derivation of the MRP-equivalent poverty lines for 2011-12 corresponding to the MMRP-based poverty lines proposed by this Expert Group (Rangarajan) makes it possible to derive the corresponding poverty lines for 2004-05 as well. These turn out to be, ₹475 for Rural India and ₹749 for Urban India. And, the corresponding poverty ratios for 2004-05 are: 47.7 per cent (41.8% as per Tendulkar Methodology) for Rural India; and, 42.5 per cent (25.7% as per Tendulkar Methodology); and, 46.2 per cent (37.2%) for the country as a whole. It is important to emphasize that, the percentage point decline in HCRs over the period 2004-05–2011-12 are not markedly different under the two methodologies: a reduction of 16.7 percentage points as per the Rangarajan methodology compared to a reduction of 15.3 percentage points as per the current official poverty lines.

Dis-aggregation of National Poverty Line into State-Specific Poverty Lines

The poverty lines in 2011-12 at the national level are expressed as monthly per capita consumption expenditure of ₹972 in rural areas and ₹1407 in urban areas, both at 2011-12 prices. These poverty lines are estimated from the MMRP consumption expenditure distribution of NSS 68th Round. These national level poverty lines are disaggregated into state-specific poverty lines in order to reflect the inter-state price differential. The method of constructing the state-wise poverty lines from the national level poverty line in 2011-12 is broadly similar to that outlined by the Expert Group (Tendulkar) and is described below.

Implicit prices for several commodity and commodity groups namely cereals, pulses, milk, oil, egg, fish, meat, vegetables, fresh fruit, dry fruit, sugar, salt, spices, other-food, intoxicants, fuel and light, clothing, bedding and footwear are calculated from their quantity and value of consumption gathered in NSS consumer expenditure data of the 68th Round (2011-12). From these, state relative to all-India Fisher price index has been computed, separately in rural and urban areas. For the remaining items for which the prices could not be computed from the NSS consumer expenditure data, a similar price differential is assumed. These items include: entertainment, personal care items, miscellaneous goods and services, durables, education and health services.

Using the Fisher index, the inter-state price differential is calculated separately in rural and urban areas and from these the national poverty lines (separately in rural and urban areas) in 2011-12 are disaggregated into state-specific poverty lines. The state-specific poverty lines in rural and urban areas derived in this manner for the year 2011-12 is given in Table 12.

Table 12

State-wise Poverty Line in Rural and Urban Areas for 2011-12—Based on Proposed Methodology

(₹ per capita, per month)

S. No	*States/UTs*	*Poverty Line*	
		Rural	*Urban*
1	Andhra Pradesh	1031.74	1370.84
2	Arunachal Pradesh	1151.01	1482.94
3	Assam	1006.66	1420.12

4	Bihar	971.28	1229.30
5	Chhattisgarh	911.80	1229.72
6	Delhi	1492.46	1538.09
7	Goa	1200.60	1470.07
8	Gujarat	1102.83	1507.06
9	Haryana	1127.82	1528.31
10	Himachal Pradesh	1066.60	1411.59
11	Jammu & Kashmir	1044.48	1403.25
12	Jharkhand	904.02	1272.06
13	Karnataka	975.43	1373.28
14	Kerala	1054.03	1353.68
15	Madhya Pradesh	941.70	1340.28
16	Maharashtra	1078.34	1560.38
17	Manipur	1185.19	1561.77
18	Meghalaya	1110.67	1524.37
19	Mizoram	1231.03	1703.93
20	Nagaland	1229.83	1615.78
21	Orissa	876.42	1205.37
22	Punjab	1127.48	1479.27
23	Rajasthan	1035.97	1406.15
24	Sikkim	1126.25	1542.67
25	Tamil Nadu	1081.94	1380.36
26	Tripura	935.52	1376.55
27	Uttar Pradesh	889.82	1329.55
28	Uttarakhand	1014.95	1408.12
29	West Bengal	934.10	1372.68
30	Puducherry#	1130.10	1382.31
31	Andaman & Nicobar Islands#	1314.98	1797.69
32	Chandigarh#	1303.17	1481.21
33	Dadra & Nagar Haveli#	1008.39	1540.81
34	Daman & Diu#	1200.60	1434.93
35	Lakshadweep#	1327.77	1458.69
	All India	972	1407

Estimation of Poverty Ratio

The state-specific poverty ratios in rural and urban areas for the year 2011-12 are calculated from the state-specific poverty lines (in rural and urban areas for the year 2011-12 as estimated above) and the state-specific distribution of persons by expenditure groups MMRP obtained from the NSS 68th Round (2011-12) large sample survey on household consumer expenditure of the National Sample Survey Office (NSSO).

The NSS consumption distribution is used as it is, that is without taking cognizance of its difference with the NAS (National Accounts Statistics) consumption. This is in line with the conclusions of our analysis of the divergence between the two sets of estimates and represents a continuation of the approach of the Expert Group (Lakdawala) and of the Expert Group (Tendulkar. The aggregate poverty ratio for the state is worked out by combining its rural and urban poverty ratios. The number of poor is estimated from the projected population of the year and the poverty ratio. The national poverty ratio is computed as an average (population weighted) of state-wise poverty ratios. The state-specific poverty ratio and number of poor estimated using the Expert Group (Rangarajan) method for the year 2011-12 is given in Table 13.

Table 13

Poverty Ratio and Number of Poor in 2011-12—
Based on Proposed Methodology

S. No.	*States/UTs*	*Rural*		*Urban*		*Total*	
		% age of Persons	*No. of Persons (lakhs)*	*% age of Persons*	*No. of Persons (lakhs)*	*% age of Persons*	*No. of Persons (lakhs)*
1	Andhra Pradesh	12.7	71.5	15.6	45.7	13.7	117.3
2	Arunachal Pradesh	39.3	4.3	30.9	1.0	37.4	5.3
3	Assam	42.0	114.1	34.2	15.4	40.9	129.5
4	Bihar	40.1	376.8	50.8	61.4	41.3	438.1
5	Chhattisgarh	49.2	97.9	43.7	26.9	47.9	124.8
6	Delhi	11.9	0.5	15.7	26.3	15.6	26.7

7	Goa	1.4	0.1	9.1	0.8	6.3	0.9
8	Gujarat	31.4	109.8	22.2	58.9	27.4	168.8
9	Haryana	11.0	18.4	15.3	14.0	12.5	32.4
10	Himachal Pradesh	11.1	6.9	8.8	0.6	10.9	7.5
11	Jammu & Kashmir	12.6	11.7	21.6	7.6	15.1	19.3
12	Jharkhand	45.9	117.0	31.3	25.5	42.4	142.5
13	Karnataka	19.8	74.8	25.1	60.9	21.9	135.7
14	Kerala	7.3	12.3	15.3	26.0	11.3	38.3
15	Madhya Pradesh	45.2	241.4	42.1	86.3	44.3	327.8
16	Maharashtra	22.5	139.9	17.0	88.4	20.0	228.3
17	Manipur	34.9	6.7	73.4	6.3	46.7	12.9
18	Meghalaya	26.3	6.4	16.7	1.0	24.4	7.4
19	Mizoram	33.7	1.8	21.5	1.2	27.4	3.1
20	Nagaland	6.1	0.8	32.1	1.9	14.0	2.8
21	Orissa	47.8	169.0	36.3	26.0	45.9	195.0
22	Punjab	7.4	12.9	17.6	18.7	11.3	31.6
23	Rajasthan	21.4	112.0	22.5	39.5	21.7	151.5
24	Sikkim	20.0	0.9	11.7	0.2	17.8	1.1
25	Tamil Nadu	24.3	91.1	20.3	72.8	22.4	163.9
26	Tripura	22.5	6.1	31.3	3.2	24.9	9.3
27	Uttar Pradesh	38.1	600.9	45.7	208.2	39.8	809.1
28	Uttarakhand	12.6	8.9	29.5	9.4	17.8	18.4
29	West Bengal	30.1	188.6	29.0	86.8	29.7	275.4
30	Puducherry	5.9	0.2	8.6	0.7	7.7	1.0
31	Andaman & Nicobar Islands#	6.6	0.2	4.9	0.1	6.0	0.2
32	Chandigarh#	12.0	0.0	21.5	2.3	21.3	2.3
33	Dadra & Nagar Haveli#	55.2	1.0	15.3	0.3	35.6	1.3
34	Daman & Diu#	0.0	0.0	17.6	0.4	13.7	0.4
35	Lakshadweep#	0.6	0.0	7.9	0.0	6.5	0.0
	All India	30.9	2605.2	26.4	1024.7	29.5	3629.9

The price inflation during the period 2009-10 to 2011-12, at the state level (separately in rural and urban areas), has been calculated from the increase in the cost of the consumption basket of the poor, that is the poverty line as estimated by the Planning Commission for these two years using the Expert Group (Tendulkar) methodology. The price inflation during this period has been applied to deflate the state-wise poverty line in 2011-12 estimated above from the Expert Group (Rangarajan) methodology in order to arrive at the state-wise poverty lines for the year 2009-10. The state-wise poverty ratio for the year 2009-10 is estimated from the state-wise poverty lines for the year as estimated above and the state-wise class distribution of persons in the year as obtained from the MMRP consumption distribution of the NSS 66th Round (2009-10) consumer expenditure data. The state-wise poverty line and poverty ratio for the year 2009-10 so derived are given in Table 14 and Table 15 respectively.

Table 14

State-wise Rural and Urban Poverty Lines for 2009-10—Based on Proposed Methodology

(₹ per capita, per month)

S. No	States/UTs	Poverty Line	
		Rural	Urban
1	Andhra Pradesh	832.27	1258.09
2	Arunachal Pradesh	957.11	1294.03
3	Assam	840.87	1232.20
4	Bihar	818.77	1032.82
5	Chhattisgarh	762.55	1167.81
6	Delhi	975.02	1410.90
7	Goa	1025.70	1328.95
8	Gujarat	859.35	1244.80
9	Haryana	879.65	1275.45
10	Himachal Pradesh	827.03	1178.46
11	Jammu & Kashmir	847.57	1200.39
12	Jharkhand	744.70	1086.07
13	Karnataka	680.81	1145.52
14	Kerala	803.06	1139.81
15	Madhya Pradesh	772.29	1153.59
16	Maharashtra	829.29	1331.33

17	Manipur	923.59	1274.32
18	Meghalaya	859.02	1307.27
19	Mizoram	981.25	1385.76
20	Nagaland	985.00	1424.22
21	Orissa	715.56	1030.67
22	Punjab	888.08	1230.66
23	Rajasthan	864.49	1186.74
24	Sikkim	882.49	1302.62
25	Tamil Nadu	785.66	1179.80
26	Tripura	777.48	1171.57
27	Uttar Pradesh	768.65	1130.76
28	Uttarakhand	830.09	1169.82
29	West Bengal	767.20	1162.06
30	Puducherry#	557.05	821.03
	All India	801	1198

Table 15

Poverty Ratio and Number of Poor in 2009-10—
Based on Proposed Methodology

S. No.	States/UTs	Rural		Urban		Combined	
		%age of Persons	No. of Persons (lakhs)	%age of Persons	No. of Persons (lakhs)	%age of Persons	No. of Persons (lakhs)
1	Andhra Pradesh	27.0	151.7	30.5	83.7	28.1	235.5
2	Arunachal Pradesh	31.3	3.3	34.1	1.0	31.9	4.3
3	Assam	42.9	113.2	40.2	17.2	42.5	130.4
4	Bihar	65.1	586.4	55.0	62.6	63.9	648.9
5	Chhattisgarh	58.9	113.6	36.5	20.9	53.8	134.5
6	Delhi	4.9	0.2	24.7	39.4	24.1	39.6
7	Goa	7.2	0.4	13.1	1.2	10.8	1.6
8	Gujarat	37.0	127.1	35.6	88.7	36.4	215.8
9	Haryana	19.2	31.4	24.8	21.1	21.1	52.5
10	Himachal Pradesh	11.2	6.8	22.5	1.5	12.3	8.3
11	Jammu & Kashmir	14.4	12.9	32.4	10.7	19.2	23.6
12	Jharkhand	55.3	135.9	42.1	32.4	52.1	168.4

contd...

...contd

13	Karnataka	24.3	90.5	26.7	61.4	25.2	151.8
14	Kerala	9.7	17.4	23.7	35.4	16.0	52.7
15	Madhya Pradesh	51.3	265.1	45.0	88.3	49.6	353.4
16	Maharashtra	27.6	168.1	30.3	150.8	28.8	318.8
17	Manipur	44.4	8.3	76.7	6.1	54.1	14.4
18	Meghalaya	25.8	6.0	36.8	2.1	28.0	8.1
19	Mizoram	29.9	1.6	24.8	1.4	27.3	2.9
20	Nagaland	11.1	1.6	37.2	2.0	18.3	3.6
21	Orissa	50.0	172.7	41.2	28.2	48.5	200.9
22	Punjab	14.8	25.5	28.6	29.0	20.0	54.6
23	Rajasthan	31.9	161.6	38.5	64.1	33.5	225.7
24	Sikkim	25.0	1.1	16.7	0.2	23.1	1.4
25	Tamil Nadu	25.9	95.7	29.7	101.4	27.7	197.1
26	Tripura	16.2	4.4	31.7	2.9	20.1	7.3
27	Uttar Pradesh	46.3	706.5	49.6	215.1	47.0	921.6
28	Uttarakhand	22.5	15.6	36.4	10.9	26.7	26.5
29	West Bengal	37.8	233.1	36.6	104.0	37.4	337.1
30	A & N Islands	4.0	0.1	5.3	0.1	4.4	0.2
31	Chandigarh	10.3	0.0	12.3	1.2	12.3	1.3
32	Dadra & N. Haveli	65.4	1.2	37.3	0.5	53.0	1.7
33	Daman & Diu	24.6	0.2	55.8	0.9	47.1	1.1
34	Lakshadweep	4.2	0.01	10.8	0.1	9.2	0.1
35	Puducherry	3.2	0.1	4.6	0.4	4.2	0.5
	All India	39.6	3259.3	35.1	1286.9	38.2	4546.2

Notes:
1. Population as on 1st March 2010 has been used for estimating number of persons below poverty line. (Interpolated between 2001 and 2011 population census)
2. Poverty line of Tamil Nadu is used for Andaman and Nicobar Island.
3. Urban Poverty Line of Punjab is used for both rural and urban areas of Chandigarh.
4. Poverty Line of Maharashtra is used for Dadra & Nagar Haveli
5. Poverty line of Goa is used for Daman & Diu.
6. Poverty Line of Kerala is used for Lakshadweep.

The estimate of poverty ratio for the years 2009-10 and 2011-12 derived from the Expert Group (Rangarajan) methodology and Tendulkar methodology are summarised in Table 16.

Table 16

Poverty Estimates in 2009-10 and 2011-12

	Year	Poverty Ratio			No. of poor (million)		
		Rural	Urban	Total	Rural	Urban	Total
		Expert Group (Rangarajan)					
1.	2009-10	39.6	35.1	38.2	325.9	128.7	454.6
2.	2011-12	30.9	26.4	29.5	260.5	102.5	363.0
3.	Reduction (%age points)	8.7	8.7	8.7	65.4	26.2	91.6
		Expert Group (Tendulkar)					
1.	2009-10	33.8	20.9	29.8	278.2	76.5	354.7
2.	2011-12	25.7	13.7	21.9	216.7	53.1	269.8
3.	Reduction (%age points)	8.1	7.2	7.9	61.5	23.4	84.9

A comparison of the poverty ratio for the two years 2009-10 and 2011-12 derived from the Expert Group (Rangarajan) method and the Expert Group (Tendulkar) method shows that the average level of poverty ratio derived from the Expert Group (Rangarajan) method is higher than that derived from the Expert Group (Tendulkar) method. The all-India poverty ratio derived from the Expert Group (Rangarajan) method is 8.4 percentage points higher in 2009-10 and 7.6 percentage points higher in 2011-12 than that derived by the Planning Commission using the Expert Group (Tendulkar) method. Though Rangarajan Committee methodology gives higher level of absolute poverty ratio, the reduction in poverty ratio from Rangarajan method is not very different than that of Tendulkar method. As MMRP based MPCE distribution is not available for the year 2004-05, poverty ratio for 2004-05 based on Rangarajan methodology cannot be directly estimated.

Updating the Poverty Line for Later Years

The updating of the poverty line constructed for the year 2011-12 for inflation in the coming years require appropriate price index numbers so that we are able to preserve the real value of the PLB for 2011-12. Our review of methodologies adopted by the 1979 Task Force and the Lakdawala and Tendulkar Expert Groups in Chapter 3 points to a continuing need to allow for changing consumption patterns, which, in turn, requires the use of "Ideal Index numbers" such as the Fisher Index to capture the "true" inflation faced by the population. In this context it may be noted that a rise in the share of food grains sourced by households from the Public Distribution System—which may gain pace as the National Food Security Act gets implemented– will be an important element of the changing composition of private consumption expenditure.

The use of Fisher index will require the weighting diagrams for both the base year and the terminal year, and, this can be drawn, as at present, from the large-sample NSS Consumer Expenditure Surveys. The next requirement for the construction of Fisher indices is a set of price-relatives, at least for the major item-groups in the consumption basket. Recently, the Central Statistical Office (CSO) has started compiling the consumer price index at the state level for rural and urban areas. These state-wise price indices are available at a disaggregated level of commodity groups such as food, beverages and tobacco, fuel and light, housing (for urban areas only), clothing, bedding and footwear, and miscellaneous items from 2011. We could use the published price-indices for the listed item–groups for the construction of Fisher indices. Note, however, that with such highly aggregated item-groups, the impact of within-group changes in the composition of expenditures will not be captured. This is particularly problematic for the price indices for Food as a single item-group since the weighting diagram underlying the currently available CSO consumer price indices relate to 2004-05. For the Food –group, therefore, the Expert Group (Rangarajan) recommends that the current practice of relying on the unit values derivable from the NSSO Consumer Expenditure Surveys should continue till such time a new CPI with a weighting diagram based on the 2011-12 pattern of consumption becomes available. In respect of non-food-items, the price indices available in the exiting CSO Consumer Price Indices can be used in the construction of requisite Fisher indices.

Once the new series of Consumer Price Index numbers (with 2011-12 as the base year) become available, there will be a trade–off between the operational convenience of using these price indices as they are readily available and the desirability of using "Ideal Price

Indices" for capturing true inflation. A resolution of this trade –off will depend on an assessment of the extent of change in the structure of consumption at that point in time relative to the 2011-12 structure of consumption.

The procedure outlined above can be used to revise the state-wise poverty line for 2011-12 for subsequent years and, thereafter, compute state-level poverty ratios for later years.

Annexure C-1

Share of Different Commodity Groups in PLB, 2011-12 (percentage)

S. No.	*Items Groups*	*Rural*	*Urban*
1	Cereals & substitute	14.6	10.3
2	Pulses & products	3.5	3.0
3	Milk & milk products	6.3	6.4
4	Salt & sugar	2.0	1.7
5	Edible oil	4.5	3.8
6	Egg, fish & meat	4.8	4.0
7	Vegetables	8.4	6.0
8	Fruits	1.7	2.1
9	Spices	3.9	3.3
10	Other food	7.2	6.1
	Food total	57.0	46.7
11	*Pan*, tobacco & intoxicants	2.9	2.1
12	Fuel and light	9.7	7.9
13	Medical (Instt & non-instt)	4.5	3.4
14	Conveyance	3.6	7.3
15	Rent	0.1	5.3
16	Clothing & bedding	7.8	8.3
17	Footwear	1.0	0.9
18	Education	3.0	8.1
19	Durable goods	1.9	1.5
20	Other non-food	8.5	8.6
	Non-food Total	43.0	53.3
	Total MPCE-Poverty Line	972.30	1406.96

Annexure C-2

Locating the Poverty Line: An Alternate Approach by Mahesh Vyas

1. Mahesh Vyas, Managing Director, Centre for Monitoring Indian Economy (CMIE), deployed the detailed household survey data collected by CMIE from a large panel of over 150,000 randomly selected households to determine the poverty line empirically. This empirical estimation rests on a simple definition of poverty and the advantage of a household survey that captures both, household income and household expenses simultaneously from all sample households.
2. Poverty is defined here as the inability of a household to meet its current consumption expenses with its current incomes. In this approach there is no need to define a minimum consumption basket of the poor. Households make their own decisions regarding their consumption within the constraints of their budgets and the environment of their dwelling. Minimum requirements vary across different environments and over time and seasons. The simple poverty definition stated above allows us to let households make their choices and we infer from these observations, what the poverty line should be.
3. Exceptions apart, it is axiomatic that households first meet all their basic requirements (no matter how they perceive these) before they save. It is also axiomatic that again, exceptions apart, households do not choose to live beyond their means. Households either balance their expenses against their income or they leave some surplus. Therefore, poverty can also be defined as the inability of a household to save.
4. Households whose incomes are insufficient to meet expenses and who cannot either raise incomes or curtail expenses, borrow to bridge the shortfall of their income. At the lower end of the spectrum of incomes, such borrowing is expected to be the last resort, because for these households, borrowings increase the probability of falling into a debt trap. If the unit of time measurement in this empirical exercise is a year, then the borrowing is also not to smoothen consumption in the face of a

seasonal fall in income. This borrowing is mostly a borrowing to overcome a very basic deprivation.

5. The point at which a household decides to borrow to keep current consumption expenses above current income is a decision that a household makes. By observing the behavior of households, we can derive the point at which the incomes are insufficient. This would be an empirical derivation rather than an arbitrary imposition. This can be derived if a household survey measures both income and expenses.
6. CMIE's Consumer Pyramids survey does capture both, household income and household expenses (besides several other indicators) for a randomly selected and representative panel of about 150,000 households in India. The survey is conducted repeatedly over the entire panel during a year to capture the impact of seasonality on household well-being. Data for fiscal 2011-12 was captured over four full surveys over the entire panel between July 2011 and June 2012.
7. The household income data captured by CMIE in its Consumer Pyramids survey includes income earned by every member of the household. Income includes four kinds of income: (a) regular income such as wages or the regular earnings of a business household or the farming income of a farmers household, (b) other income, which includes rents, dividends, interest and other non-regular sources of income such as bonuses, etc., (c) transfer incomes, which include pensions, subsidies paid to households, compensation for calamities, and private transfers, and (d) imputed income which is the value of goods produced by the household for internal consumption.
8. Household expenses include all expenses on food, intoxicants, clothing and footwear, cosmetics and toiletries, restaurant expenses, recreation, bills & rents, power & fuel, transport services, communication & information, education, health and miscellaneous expenses. The complete schedule includes over a hundred expense items.
9. The poverty line can be found by creating a series of households with their income and corresponding expenses, ordered by their

income. This can therefore be imagined as a paired series of households arranged in ascending order of their income, along with their corresponding expenses. In such a series, at the lower end of the spectrum of incomes, most households would show incomes that are lower than their expenses and at the higher end of the spectrum, households would have income that are much in excess of their expenses. The point of intersection where income equals expenses, is the poverty line. Below this point of intersection, households are unable to meet their expenses and above this point, they are.

10. However, before such a point of intersection is determined, we must adjust the household incomes and expenses observed in CMIE's Consumer Pyramids database for the purpose of poverty estimations. These adjustments are described below:

11. Income is an important measure of well-being but, it is an incomplete measure of well-being. Income delivers fewer capabilities to the under-privileged than it does to those who are better endowed. It is therefore necessary to adjust the income of a household downwards if the household has no literate member, no assets and no tapped water. The argument is that the worth of a rupee in the hands of a household that has no literate person is a lot less than it is in the hands of a household that has at least one literate. Therefore, income of households as observed in the Consumer Pyramids survey with no literate member is reduced by ten per cent for the purpose of locating the poverty line. Similarly, a rupee in the hands of a household with no assets is worth a lot less compared to a household with at least some assets. Here again, the observed income of households that have no assets is reduced by ten per cent. The same is true in the case of a household that has no tapped water.

12. The above-mentioned adjustment of income is in a way, a means of incorporating some multi-dimensional aspects of poverty, such as illiteracy, lack of access of assets and tapped water. The adjustments to income for these are admittedly arbitrary and should be refined in future, possibly with controlled experiments to find the impact of each of these on the ability of income to deliver capabilities.

13. Expenses need to be adjusted to provide for a minimum health and education expense and for a minimum liquidity in hand.
14. Households that are vulnerable because of their low incomes are likely to cut back on expenses in general. Beyond a point, a household would not be able to cutback expenses on food. It will find its own minimum requirement of food and then if required it may borrow. Cutbacks on other expenses heads such as intoxicants, entertainment, some clothing and footwear, cosmetics and toiletries and other miscellaneous expenses are easier. Curtailing these expenses also does not cause long-term damage to the household. However, a cutback of expenses on health and education can be severely debilitating as these directly curtail the ability of the household to raise income. It is thus necessary that households do receive a minimum health service and a minimum education. Given that these services are not freely available as public goods for all practical purposes, they imply a minimum expenditure.
15. But, households may choose to cut back on health and education expenses under adverse conditions and not treat these as necessities as say, food. They may not borrow, for example, to ensure good health and education as they may to ensure food intake. It is likely that households make more than an acceptable cut in expenses on health and education. It is likely that the health of only the earning member is given attention or only one of multiple children is educated. Such a situation is considered unacceptable in this attempt to find a poverty line.
16. To offset such unacceptable behavior that arises essentially because of poverty, it is proposed that every household should be allocated an expenditure budget on health and education that is not less than the median expenditure on health and education in their respective states. Thus, the required expenses of a household are raised on the health and education accounts for the purpose of this exercise to match up to the median expenses for the state, if these are below the median.
17. A household that is able to just about meet its current consumption expenses through its current incomes faces considerable

unmitigated risk. Vulnerability to sudden emanation of normally avoidable risk is also a manifestation of deprivation. There are at least three risks that a household should be able to finance through its current income. These are the ability to finance the time-lag between income and expenses, the non-seasonal volatility of expenses and expenses caused by emergencies. These can be mitigated essentially by the availability of some liquidity.

18. The time-lag between income and expenses arises because, for example, wages may be paid at the end of a month, but expenses are incurred every day from the beginning of the month. The poor are particularly vulnerable to delays in receiving payments due to them. In effect, a household near the poverty line needs to maintain a nearly one-month credit for supplies. Since the cost of finance for the poor is high, this can turn out to be equivalent to about a week's income. This needs to be financed from current income.

19. The non-seasonal volatility of expenses needs to be mitigated necessarily through current income. Non-seasonal volatility of expenses is caused essentially by inflation. Therefore, current income needs to be marked up by a proportion equivalent to the average monthly rate of inflation to offset the risk associated with a sudden jump in prices.

20. Also, there is a need for every household to save. The poor in particular, need to save to be able to finance a sudden unanticipated large expenditure. The poor also need to save to come out of poverty. A saving that is equivalent to one month's income may be considered to be reasonable. It may not be adequate to mitigate the shortfall in income because we do not know what is adequate. But, it is reasonable to assume that a typical household should save of the order of one month's income, which is about 8.3 per cent of the annual income.

21. In light of the above, it may be reasonable (though not necessarily adequate) to assume that annual expenses need to be marked up by about 10 per cent to provide liquidity to mitigate some of the risks faced by households whose adjusted incomes are close to current expenses.

22. To summarise, adjusted income is nominal stated income of a household that is adjusted down-wards by ten per cent each for the lack of literacy, tapped water and assets. Adjusted expenses are the total nominal stated expenses of a household adjusted upwards to include at least the median expenditure on health and education and upwards ten per cent to provide the minimum liquidity.

Deriving the Poverty Level from Survey Data

22. Poverty is defined as the insufficiency of the adjusted income to meet the adjusted expenses during a year. If we assume that households with very low adjusted incomes find such incomes insufficient to meet their adjusted consumption expenses and, as incomes rise, households find it easier to meet their adjusted consumption expenses through their adjusted current incomes, then the poverty line can be the point in a vector of households ordered by adjusted income at which adjusted income is equal to the adjusted consumption expenses.
23. Using Consumer Pyramids survey data of 2011-12, a series of households that are ordered by their adjusted income with observations of adjusted income and adjusted expenses for each household in 2011-12 was created. Adjusted expenses of households with lower incomes were found to be higher than their corresponding adjusted incomes and, adjusted expenses of households with higher incomes were lower than their corresponding adjusted expenses. The two series therefore intersect.
24. However, as expected, this intersection was not unique. A number of thrifty poor at the lower end of the spectrum and extravagant rich at the upper end of the spectrum ensured that there was no unique point of intersection of the two series. And so, a number of centered simple moving average (SMA) series were created to find the appropriate smoothing to remove the noise of exceptional households. SMAs of 0.25 per cent, 0.50 per cent, 0.75 per cent, 1 per cent, 1.25 per cent and 1.50 per cent of the sample size were generated to find a unique point of intersection of the two series.

25. As the SMA period increases, the smallest thrifty poor rises to a higher point in the series and the most extravagant rich falls to a lower point in the series. And, at some SMA level the smallest thrifty poor and the most extravagant rich converge. This point of convergence yields the poverty level.

Simple moving average	*Rural*		*Urban*		*India*	
	Thrifty poor	*Extravagant rich*	*Thrifty poor*	*Extravagant rich*	*Thrifty poor*	*Extravagant rich*
Actual	200	27722	420	32118	200	32118
0.25% HHs	798	1251	1119	2500	859	1501
0.50% HHs	846	1092	1232	2003	894	1131
0.75% HHs	884	1091	1234	1365	891	1098
1.00% HHs	888	1010	1230	1319	957	1095
1.25% HHs	888	1011	1226	1297	960	1093
1.50% HHs	885	1010	1282	1282	963	1019

26. The convergence is perfect in the case of urban India. But, in the case of rural India, the convergence is not complete even at a moving average of 1.5 per cent of the households. Given that the values have stabilised without convergence, we make a choice of the upper bound of ₹1,010 of monthly per capita income (which is the same as the monthly per capita expenses because this is the point of intersection of the two series) as the poverty line in rural India. The choice for urban India is unambiguous in this respect at ₹1,282 of monthly per capita income.

No. M-11019/2/2012-PP

Planning Commission

(Perspective Planning Division)

Yojana Bhavan, Sansad Marg,
New Delhi, 5th June, 2012

Order

Subject: Expert Group to Review the Methodology for Measurement of Poverty.

The methodology for estimation of poverty followed by the Planning Commission has been based on the recommendations made by Working Group/Task Force/Expert Groups consisting of eminent experts in the field of poverty. The Planning Commission has constituted these Groups from time to time to revisit the methodological issues relating to the measurement of poverty so as to make the estimates more relevant to the contemporary economic situation. The last such Group was constituted in 2005 under the chairmanship of Prof. Suresh Tendulkar whose recommendations are being used by the Planning Commission to estimate poverty at present.

2. It has now been decided to set up an Expert Group under the Chairmanship of Dr. C. Rangarajan, Chairman, Prime Minister's Economy Advisory Council. The composition of the Group is as under:

1.	Dr. C. Rangarajan, Chairman Prime Minister's Economy Advisory Council	**Chairman**
2.	Dr. Mahendra Dev, Director, Indira Gandhi Institute of Development Research	**Member**
3.	Dr. K. Sundaram, Former Prof, Delhi School of Economics	**Member**
4.	Dr. Mahesh Vyas, MD & CEO Centre for Monitoring Indian Economy	**Member**
5.	K.L. Datta, Former Adviser (Perspective Planning), Planning Commission	**Member Convener**

3. The Terms of Reference for the Expert Group are as under:

   i. "To comprehensively review the existing methodology of estimation of poverty and examine whether the poverty line should be fixed solely in terms of a consumption basket or whether other criteria are also relevant, and if so, whether the two can be effectively combined to evolve a basis for estimation of poverty in rural and urban areas.

ii. To examine the issue of divergence between consumption estimates based on the NSSO methodology and those emerging from the National Accounts aggregates; and to suggest a methodology for updating consumption poverty lines using the new consumer price indices launched by the CSO for rural and urban areas state-wise.

iii. To review alternative methods of estimation of poverty which may be in use in other countries, including their procedural aspects; and indicate whether on this basis, a particular method can be evolved for empirical estimation of poverty in India, including procedures for updating it over time and across states.

iv. To recommend how the estimates of poverty, as evolved above, should be linked to eligibility and entitlements for schemes and programmes under the Government of India".

4. The Chairman of the Working Group may co-opt any other official/ non-official expert/representative of any organization as a member (s), if required and may form sub-group (s) to address specific issues.

5. Adviser (Perspective Planning), Planning Commission would serve as the secretariat for the Expert Group and maintain all requisite records.

6. The expenditure of the members on TA/DA in connection with the meetings, field visits and other necessary travels of the Working Group/Sub-Group will be borne by the parent Department/ Ministry/Organization. The TA/DA expenditure in respect of non-official members will be borne by the Planning Commission as admissible to the Class–I officers to the Government of India.

7. The Expert Group will submit its report to the Planning Commission within a year.

(Savita Sharma)
Adviser (PPD)
Telefax: 23096786

Bibliography

Alkire, Sabina and Maria Emma Santos (2010). *Multidimensional Poverty Index*. Oxford Poverty and Human Development Initiative. July.

Anand, Sudhir, and Amartya Sen (1997). "Concepts of Human Development and Poverty: A Multidimensional Perspective", in *Human Development Papers*. United Nations Development Programme.

Atkinson, Anthony B. (1987). "On the Measurement of Poverty", *Econometrica* 55: 749-764.

———. (1998). *Poverty in Europe*. Oxford: Blackwell Press.

Banerjee, Abhijit and Esther Duflo (2007). "The Economic Lives of the Poor", *Journal of Economic Perspectives* 21(2): 141-67.

Bhargava, Alok, Aravinda M. Guntupalli and Michael Lokshin (2011). "Health Care Utilization, Socioeconomic Factors and Child Health in India", in *J. Biosoc. Sci*.

Bhalla, S.S. (2003a). "Recounting the Poor, Poverty in India 1983-1999", *Economic and Political Weekly* 38(4): 338-49, 25-31 Jan.

———. (2003b). "Crying Wolf on Poverty", *Economic and Political Weekly* 38: 2843-56, 05 July-11 July.

Bhide, Shashanka and Aasha Kapur Mehta (2005). "Tracking Poverty through Panel Data: Rural Poverty in India 1970-1998", *Chronic Poverty Research Centre Working paper* No. 28. New Delhi: CPRCIIPA.

Bouis, Howard and Laurence J. Haddad (1985). "Are Estimates of Calorie-Income Elasticities Too High? A Recalibration of the Plausible Range", *Journal of Development Economics* 39: 333-64.

Coffey, D., A. Deaton, J. Dreze, D. Spears and A. Tarozzi (2013). "Stunting among Children", *Economic and Political Weekly* XLVIII(34).

Citro, Constance and Robert Michael (1995). *Measuring Poverty: A New Approach*. Washington, DC: National Academy Press.

Corazzini, Luca, Lucio Esposito and Francesca Majorano (2010). "Exploring the Absolutist Vs, Relativist Perception of Poverty Using Cross-Country Questionnaire Survey", *Journal of Economic Psychology*.

Dandekar, V.M. (1996). "Population, Poverty and Employment, The Indian Economy, 1947-92". Volume 2. New Delhi: Sage Publications.

Dandekar, V.M. and N. Rath (1971). "Poverty in India", *Economic and Political Weekly* 6(1 & 2), 9 January.

Datta, K. (2010). "Index of Poverty and Deprivation in Context of Inclusive Growth", *Indian Journal of Human Development* 4(1): 45-73.

de Mesnard, Louis (2007). "Poverty Reduction: The Paradox of the Endogenous Poverty Line", *LEG-Document de travail-Economie* 2007-05. LEG, Laboratoire d'Economie et de Gestion, CNRS UMR 5118. Université de Bourgogne.

De Vos, Klaas and Garner Thesia (1991). "An Evaluation of Subjective Poverty Definitions: Comparing Results from the U.S. and the Netherlands", *Review of Income and Wealth* 37(3): 267-85.

Deaton, Angus(2003). "Prices and Poverty in India, 1987-2000", *Economic and Political Weekly* 38(4): 362-68.

———. (2008). "Price Trends in India and their Implications for Measuring Poverty", *Economic and Political Weekly* 43(6): 43-49.

Deaton, Angus and Jean Dreze (2002). "Poverty and Inequality in India: A Re-examination", *Economic and Political Weekly*: 3729-48, 7 September.

———. (2009). *Food and Nutrition in India.*

Deaton. Angus and V. Kozel (2005). "Data and Dogma: The Great Indian Poverty Debate", *The World Bank Research Observer* 20(2) Fall.

Dev, S. Mahendra (2005). "Calorie Norms and Poverty", *Economic & Political Weekly* 40(8): 789-92.

Dhamija, N. and S. Bhide (2009). "Dynamics of Chronic Poverty: Variations in Factors Influencing Entry and Exit of Chronic Poor", *CPRC-IIPA, Working Paper* No. 39.

Expert Group of the Indian Council of Medical Research 2009). *Nutrient Requirements and Recommended Dietary Allowances for Indians.*

Foster, J., S. Seth, M. Lokshinand Z. Sajaia (n.d.). *A Unified Approach to Measuring Poverty and Inequality: Theory and Practice.* Streamlined Analysis With Adept Software. Washington D.C.: World Bank.

Foster, James E. (1998). "Absolute versus Relative Poverty", *American Economic Review, Papers and Proceedings* 88(2): 335-41.

Gaiha, R. (1989). "Are the Chronically Poor also the Poorest in Rural India?", *Development and Change* 20.

Gaiha, R. and A.B. Deolaliker (1993). "*Persistent, Expected and innate Poverty: Estimates for Semi-Arid Rural South India*", *Cambridge Journal of Economics* 17(4): 409-21.

Gangopadhyay, K. and K. Singh (2013). "Extent of Poverty in India: A Different Dimension", *Economic and Political Weekly* XLVIII(6), 9 February.

Gasparini, L. (2004). *Poverty and Inequality in Argentina: Methodological Issues and Literature Review.* CEDLAS, Universidad Nacional de La Plata.

Ghosh, Jayati (2009). "Global Crisis and the Indian Economy" in *Global Financial Crisis: Impact on India's Poor—Some Initial Perspectives.* United Nations Development Programme India. Viewed on 26 December 2011.

Government of India (1979). *Report of the Task Force on Projection of Minimum Needs and Effective Consumption Demands.*

———. (1979a). "Survey Results: Consumer Expenditure: NSS, 27th Round (October1972-September 1973)", *Sarvekshana:* S287-S436. Journal of the National Sample Survey Oganisation, Department of Statistics, Ministry of Planning.

———. (1983). "A Note on Per Capita Per Day Intake of Calories, Protein and Fat based on the Data Collected in the Household Survey on Consumer Expenditure, NSS 27th Round: October 1972-September 1973', *Sarvekshana* VI(3-4).

———. (1986a). "Some Results on the Second Quinquennial Survey on Consumer Expenditure: National Sample Survey Thirty-second round (July '77-June '78)", *Sarvekshana* IX(3): S51-S184.

———. (1986b). "A Report on the Third Quinquennial Survey on Consumer Expenditure: National Sample Survey 38th Round (January-December 1983)", *Sarvekshana* IX(4): S1-S102.

———. (1989a). "Results on Per Capita Consumption of Cereals for Various Sections of Population: NSS 38th Round (1983)", *Sarvekshana* XIII(2): S1-S176.

———. (1989b). "Results on Per Capita and Per Consumer Unit Per Diem Intake of Calorie, Protein and Fat and Perceptions of the People on Adequacy of Food", *Sarvekshana* XIII(2, Issue No. 41): S177-S258.

———. (1991). "Results of the Fourth Quinquennial Survey on Consumer Expenditure (Sub-sample 1): NSS 43rd Round (July 1987-June 1988)", *Sarvekshana* XV(1).

———. (1993). *Report of the Expert Group on Estimation of Proportion and Number of Poor.*

———. (1996a). *Level and Pattern of Consumer Expenditure: 5th Quinquennial Survey 1993-94.* Report No. 402. New Delhi: National Sample Survey Organisation, Department of Statistics.

———. (1996b). "Nutritional Intake in India: NSS 50th Round July 1993-June 1994", *Fifth Quinquennial Survey on Consumer Expenditure.* Report No. 405. New Delhi: National Sample Survey Organisation, Department of Statistics.

———. (2001a). *Level and Pattern of Consumer Expenditure in India 1999- 2000.* NSS 55th Round July 1999-June 2000. Report No. 457 (55/1.0/3). New Delhi: National Sample Survey Organisation, Ministry of Statistics & Programme Implementation.

———. (2001b). *Reported Adequacy of Food Intake in India 1999-2000.* NSS 55th Round (July 1999-June 2000). Report No. 466(55/1.0/7). New Delhi: National Sample Survey Organisation.

———. (2001c). *Nutritional Intake in India 1999-2000.* NSS 55th Round (July 1999-June 2000). Report No. 471(55/1.0/9). New Delhi: National Sample Survey Organisation.

———. (2006a). *Morbidity, Health Care and the Condition of the Aged.* NSS 60th Round (January-June 2004). Report No. 507(60/25.0/1). New Delhi: National Sample Survey Organisation.

———. (2006b). *Level and Pattern of Consumer Expenditure, 2004-05.* NSS 61st Round (July 2004-June 2005). NSS Report No. 508(61/1.0)/1). New Delhi: National Sample Survey Organisation, Ministry of Statistics and Programme Implementation.

———. (2007a). *Perceived Adequacy of Food Consumption In Indian Households 2004-05.* NSS 61st Round (July 2004-June 2005). Report No. 512(61/1.0/5). New Delhi: National Sample Survey Organisation.

———. (2007c). *Nutritional Intake in India 2004-05.* NSS 61st Round (July 2004-June 2005). Report No. 513(61/1.0/6). New Delhi: National Sample Survey Organisation.

———. (2009). *Report of the Expert Group to Review the Methodology for Estimation of Poverty.* Chaired by S.D. Tendulkar.

Greer, Joel and Erik Thorbecke (1986). "A Methodology for Measuring Food Poverty Applied to Kenya", *Journal of Development Economics* 24: 59-74.

Groedhart, T., V. Halberstadt, A. Kapteyn and B. van Praag (1977). "The Poverty Line: Concept and Measurement", *Journal of Human Resources* 12: 503-20.

Hagenaars, Aldi and Bernard van Praag (1985). "A Synthesis of Poverty Line Definitions", *Review of Income and Wealth* 31(2): 139-54.

Haub, C and O.P. Sharma (2010). *What Is Poverty, Really? The Case of India.* Population Reference Bureau.

Himanshu (2010). 'Towards New Poverty Lines for India', *Economic and Political Weekly* 45(1), 2-8 January.

Jain, L.R. and Suresh D. Tendulkar (1990). "Rural Poverty and its Alleviation in India: A Critical Scrutiny", *Economic and Political Weekly* XXV(38), 22 September.

———. (1995). "Economic Reforms and Poverty", *Economic and Political Weekly* XXX(23), 10 June.

Kapteyn, Arie, P. Kooreman and R. Willemse (1988). "Some Methodological Issues in the Implementation of Subjective Poverty Definitions", *Journal of Human Resources* 23: 222–42.

Kilpatrick, Robert (1973). "The Income Elasticity of the Poverty Line", *Review of Economics and Statistics* 55(3): 327-32.

Kumar, Praduman, Mruthyunjaya and Madan M. Dey (2007). "Long-term Changes in Indian Food Basket and Nutrition", *Economic and Political Weekly* 42(35): 3567-72, 01 September.

Manna, G.C. (2007). "On Calibrating the Poverty Line for Poverty Estimation in India", *Economic & Political Weekly* XLII(30).

———. (2012). "On Some Contentious Issues of the New Poverty Line", *Economic & Political Weekly* XLVII(15).

Marjit, Sugata (2011). "Conflicting Measures of Poverty and Inadequate Saving by the Poor: The Role of Status Driven Utility Function", *Discussion Papers Series* 424. Australia: School of Economics, University of Queensland.

McKinsey Global Institute (2014). *From Poverty to Empowerment: India's Imperative for Jobs, Growth, and Effective Basic Services.* February.

Meenakshi, J.V. and Brinda Viswanathan (2005). "Calorie Deprivation in Rural India between 1983 and 1999/2000", in Angus Deaton and Valerie Kozel (eds.), *The Great Indian Poverty Debate.* New Delhi: Macmillan. pp.570-83.

———. (2013). "Estimation of Calorie Norms and Measurement of Food Intake: Some Implications for the Magnitudes of the Prevalence of Undernutrition in India", *Indian Economic Review* (Special Issue on "Perspectives on Economic Development and Policy') XLVIII(1): 167-88.

Mehta, Jaya (2004). "Poverty in India", *Alternative Economic Survey 2003-04.* New Delhi: Rainbow Publishers.

Minhas, B.S. (1988) "Validation of Large Scale Sample Survey Data: A Case of NSS Estimates of Household Consumption Expenditure", *Sankhya* A, Series B 50.

Minhas, B.S. and S.M. Kansal (1989) "Comparision of NSS and CSO Estimates of Private Consumption: Some Observations Based on 1983 Data", *The Journal of Income and Wealth* 11 (1), January.

Minhas, B.S., L.R. Jain and S.D. Tendulkar (1991). "Declining Incidence of Poverty in the 1980s: Evidence versus Artefacts", *Economic and Political Weekly* XXVI(27-28): 1673-82, 06 July.

Ministry of Rural Development (2009). *Report of the Expert Group to Advise the Ministry of Rural Development on the Methodology for Conducting the Below Poverty Line (BPL) Census for 11th Five Year Plan*. August. New Delhi.

National Economic and Social Development Board (2001). *Thailand's Official Poverty Lines.* Development Evaluation Division.

National Sample Survey Office (NSSO) (2005). "Results of a Pilot Survey on suitability of Different Reference Periods for Measuring Household Consumption" in Deaton, A. & V. Kozel (eds). *The Great Indian Poverty Debate*. Delhi: Macmillan.

———. (2010). *Housing Condition and Amenities in India, 2008–09.* 65th Round. Government of India.

———. (2011). *Key Indicators of Household Consumer Expenditure in India, 2011.* 66th Round. Government of India.

———. (2012). *Household Consumption of Various Goods and Services in India, 2012.* 66th Round. Government of India.

———. (2012a). *Nutritional Intake in India, 2012.* 66th Round. Government of India.

———. (2013). *Key Indicators of Household Consumer Expenditure in India, 2013.* 68th Round, Government of India.

Organization for Economic Co-operation and Development (OECD) (2008). *Growing Unequal? Income Distribution and Poverty in OECD Countries.* Paris.

Osberg, Lars and Kuan Xu (2008). "How Should We Measure Poverty in a Changing World? Methodological Issues and Chinese Case Study", *Review of Development Economics* 12(2): 419 41.

Oxford Department of International Development (2011). *Multidimensional Poverty Index at a Glance: India Briefing.*

Palmer-Jones, Richard and Kunal Sen (2001). "On Indian Poverty Puzzles and Statistics of Poverty", *Economic & Political Weekly* 36(3): 211-17.

Panagariya, Arvind and Megha Mukim (2013). "A Comprehensive Analysis of Poverty in India", *World Bank Policy Research Working Paper* 6714, December.

Pathak, D.C. and S. Mishra (2011). "Poverty Estimates in India: Old and New Methods, 2004-05", *Working Paper* No. WP- 2011-015. Mumbai: Indira Gandhi Institute of Development Research. August.

Patnaik, Utsa (2007). "Neoliberalism and Rural Poverty in India", *Economic and Political Weekly* 42(30), 28 July.

———. (2010). "Trends in Urban Poverty under Economic Reforms: 1993-94 to 2004-05", *Economic and Political Weekly* 45(4), 23 January.

Paul, Satya (1989). "A Model of Constructing the Poverty Line", *Journal of Development Economics* 30: 129–44.

Planning Commission (2007). *Poverty Estimates for 2004-05.* Press Release.New Delhi: Press Information Bureau, Government of India, March 21.

———. (2012). *Press Note on Poverty Estimates, 2009-10.* Government of India. 19 March.

——— (2012a). *Report of the working group on nutrition, 2012.* Government of India.

———. (2013). *Press Note on Poverty Estimates, 2011–12.* Government of India.

Rural Survey Organization of National Bureau of Statistics (n.d.). *Poverty Statistics in China, 2004.* China

Pradhan, Menno and Martin Ravallion (2000). "Measuring Poverty using Qualitative Perceptions of Consumption Adequacy", *Review of Economics and Statistics* 82: 462–71.

Radhakrishna, R. (2005). "Food and Nutrition Security of the Poor: Emerging Perspectives and Policy Issues", *Economic & Political Weekly* 40(18): 1817-21.

Rao, Shobha (2001). "Nutritional Status of the Indian Population", *Journal of Biosciences* 26(4) (Suppl.): 481–89.

Ravallion, Martin (1998). "Poverty Lines in Theory and Practice", *Living Standards Measurement Study Paper* 133. Washington DC: World Bank.

———. (2010). "Poverty Lines across the World", *World Bank Policy Research Working Paper* Number 5284, April.

Ravallion, Martin and Michael Lokshin (2006). "Testing Poverty Lines", *Review of Income and Wealth* 52(3): 399-421.

Ravallion, Martin and Shaohua Chen (2009). "Weakly Relative Poverty", *Policy Research Working Paper* 4844. Washington DC: World Bank.

Raveendran, G. (2010). "New Estimates of Poverty in India: A Critique of the Tendulkar Committee Report", *Indian Journal of Human Development* 4(1): 75-89.

Ray, Ranjan and Geoffrey Lancaster (2005). "On Setting the Poverty Line Based on Estimated Nutrient Prices", *Economic and Political Weekly* 40(01), January 01-January 07.

Saith, A. (2005). "Of Calories and Things: Reflections on Nutritional Norms, Poverty Lines and Consumption Behaviour in India", *Economic and Political Weekly* 40(43): 4611-18, 22-28 October.

Sen, Amartya (1983). "Poor, Relatively Speaking", *Oxford Economic Papers* 35(2): 153-69.

Sen, Pronab (2005). "Of Calories and Things", *Economic and Political Weekly* 40(43), 22 October .

Sen, Abhijit and Himanshu (2004). "Poverty and Inequality in India II", *Economic and Political Weekly,* 25 September.

Sharma, Savita (2004). "Poverty Estimates in India: Some Key Issues", *ERD Working Paper* No 51. Manila: Asian Development Bank.

Subramanian, A. (2003). "Con*sumption of Food and Calories: Some Implications for Nutrition and Income.* New Delhi, National Council for Applied Economic Research.

Subramanian, S. (2011). "The Poverty Line: Getting It Wrong Again", *Economic & Political Weekly* 46 48): 37-42.

Sukhatme, P. V. (1978). "Assessment of Adequacy of Diets at Different Income Levels", *Economic and Political Weekly* 13(31/33): 1373-84

———. (1981). "On Measurement of Poverty", *Economic and Political Weekly* 16(32): 1318-24.

Sundaram, K. (2003). "On Identification of Households below Poverty Line in BPL Census 2002", *Economic and Political Weekly* XXXVIII(09), 01 March.

———. (2007). "Employment and Poverty in India, 2000-2005", *Economic and Political Weekly* XLII(30), 28 July 28.

———. (2008). "Employment, Wages and Poverty in the Non-Agricultural Sector: All India, 2000-2005", *Economic and Political Weekly* XLIII(22), 31 May.

Sundaram, K. and S.D. Tendulkar (1983). "Poverty Reduction and Redistribution in Sixth Plan-Population Factor and Rural-Urban Equity", *Economic and Political Weekly* XVIII(38), 17 September.

———. (2003). "NAS-NSS Estimates of Private Consumption for Poverty Estimation", *Economic and Political Weekly* XXXVIII(04), 25 January.

———. (2003a). "Poverty among Social and Economic Groups in India in 1990s", *Economic and Political Weekly* XXXVIII(50), 13 December.

———. (2003b). "Poverty has Declined in the 1990s A Resolution of Comparability Problems in NSS Consumer Expenditure Data", *Economic and Political Weekly* 38(4): 327-37, 25-31 January.

———. (2003c). "Poverty in India in the 1990s: Revised Results for All-India and 15 Major States for 1993 94", *Economic and Political Weekly:* 4865-72, 15 November.

Suryanarayana, M.H. (1996). "Food Security and Calorie Adequacy Across States: Implications for Reform", *Journal of Indian School of Political Economy* VIII(2): 203-65.

———. (2000b). "How Real is the Secular Decline in Rural Poverty?", *Economic and Political Weekly* XXXV(25): 2129-39.

Suryanarayana, M. (2009). *Nutritional Norms for Poverty: Issues and Implications.*

Svedberg, Peter (2000). *Poverty and Under-nutrition.* London: Oxford University Press.

Swaminathan, M. (2010). "The New Poverty Line: A Methodology Deeply Flawed", *Indian Journal of Human Development* 4(1).

Tendulkar, Suresh D., K. Sundaram and L.R. Jain (1993). "Poverty in India, 1970-71 to 1988-89", *ARTEP Working Papers.* New Delhi: International Labour Organisation, Asian Regional Team for Employment Promotion.

Tilak, Jandhyala, B.G. (2009). *Household Expenditure on Education and Implications for Redefining the Poverty Line in India.*

Walker, Iain and Heather Smith (2001). *Relative Deprivation: Specification, Development, and Integration.* Cambridge: Cambridge University Press.

Wodon, Quentin (1997). "Food Energy Intake and Cost of Basic Needs: Measuring Poverty in Bangladesh", *Journal of Development Studies* 34: 66–101.

Zheng, Buhong (1997). "Aggregate Poverty Measures", *Journal of Economic Surveys* 11(2): 123-40.